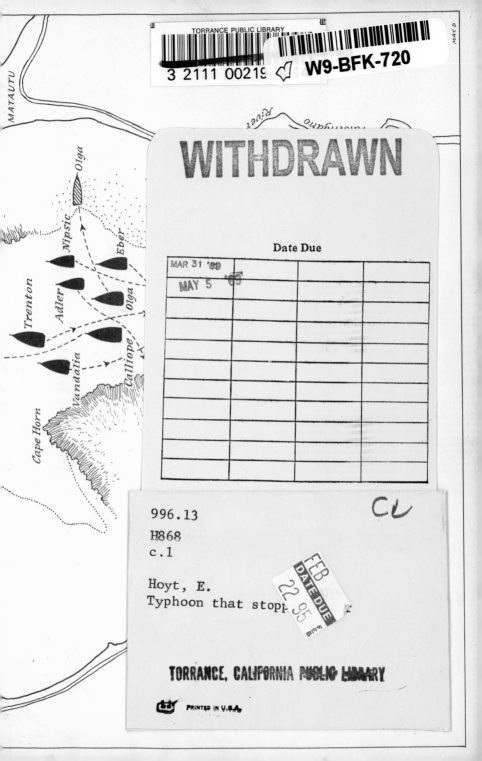

WITHDRAWN

MATAUTU

River

Olga
Nipsic
Eber
Adler
Trenton
Olga
Vandalia
Calliope
Cape Horn

Date Due

The Typhoon
That Stopped a War

BOOKS BY EDWIN P. HOYT

ADULT FICTION

A Matter of Conscience

ADULT NONFICTION

Jumbos and Jackasses
The Vanderbilts and Their Fortunes
The Supersalesmen
The Tempering Years
Spectacular Rogue: Gaston B. Means
A Gentleman of Broadway
The Golden Rot
A Short History of Science
Marilyn, the Tragic Venus
The Last Cruise of the Emden
Condition Critical, Our Hospital Crisis
The House of Morgan
Paul Robeson: The American Othello
The Army Without a Country
Alexander Woollcott: The Man Who Came to Dinner
The Guggenheims and the American Dream

JUVENILE NONFICTION

Whirlybirds, The Story of Helicopters
Heroes of the Skies
From the Turtle *to the* Nautilus
The Glorious Flattops
The Jewel Hunters
American Steamboat Stories
The Tragic Commodore, The Story of Oliver Hazard Perry
Commodore Vanderbilt
Lost Statesmen
Grover Cleveland
John Quincy Adams
Martin Van Buren
Andrew Johnson
James A. Garfield
James Knox Polk
Zachary Taylor
James Buchanan
William McKinley
The Idea Men
One Penny Black
Teddy Roosevelt in Africa

The Typhoon
That Stopped a War

by EDWIN P. HOYT

DAVID McKAY COMPANY, INC.

New York

THE TYPHOON THAT STOPPED A WAR

COPYRIGHT ©1968 BY EDWIN P. HOYT

Library of Congress Catalog Card Number: 68-18724

MANUFACTURED IN THE UNITED STATES OF AMERICA

VAN REES PRESS   •   NEW YORK

For My Wife

Contents

viii   Contents

*The Typhoon
That Stopped a War*

CHAPTER ONE

The Elements

FEBRUARY AND MARCH are the months of storm in the Samoan Islands, so during these months the islanders keep a nervous eye to north and east and do their fishing in the lagoons, close inshore, for no one knows when a typhoon will sweep across the archipelago, threatening every living creature on land and on the surface of the sea. Sometimes February carries the burden of the bad weather; sometimes it comes in March. By March 10, 1889, it appeared that the dangerous season had passed with only three serious storms having curled their way among the islands, from Suvaroff, 550 miles northeast, to New Caledonia, nearly twenty-five degrees of longitude to the west. All three typhoons had torn up coconut trees, smashed native huts, and sent pieces of roof and wooden battens sailing up the normally dusty single street of Apia, the capital, but only the storm of February 13/14 had brought real disaster. The American barkentine *Constitution* out of San Francisco had been unloading cargo in the harbor; at midnight on the thirteenth she enjoyed a moderate fresh breeze from the east, accompanied by overcast and a slight swell; twelve hours later, the *Constitution* was a wreck, lying at the bottom of Apia harbor, caught fast in the teeth of the island's coral reef.

Six warships rode easily at anchor in Apia harbor on March 10th, two ships of the United States Navy, three ships of His Germanic Majesty Kaiser Wilhelm II, and one British warship, the screw corvette H.M.S. *Calliope*. There was tension in the harbor on that morning, but it was not that of sailors making ready for a heavy blow. The tension was that of fighting men caught up in events over which they might not be able to maintain control.

The glassy calm of the harbor and the deep blue of the sky on the forenoon of March 10th contravened the thoughts running through these men's minds, for if there was anything peaceful in Samoa, it was the weather. Germany was at war with the King of Samoa, and German warships were in the harbor to enforce a state of martial law declared by the German authorities. American and British ships had come to Samoa in response to the German challenge, for the United States, in particular, was pledged to support the king. On this day America and Germany were so very close to war that the slightest incident, touched off from ship or shore, could bring the two squadrons thundering down on one another, gunports open and shot blazing.

Six naval captains sat in Apia harbor, all on edge, but not about the weather. To be sure, the night of March 7th had been nasty, the wind rising to gale force, but after that blow the pilots and old Samoa hands ashore had announced that the bad weather was at an end. The three typhoons of this year, they said, were as hard as any they had ever seen, and it was obvious that there could be no more.

On March 11th, four days after the storm of March 7th, the weather was clear and pleasant, as the last of the American squadron, the flagship U.S.S. *Trenton*, arrived in the harbor. The *Trenton* was a screw sloop of war; a bastard ship was the best one could call her, for she was of that breed caught between the old Navy and the new, rigged as a sailing ship, with a wooden hull built at the New York Navy Yard, and then given her engines and eight cylindrical boilers at the Morgan Iron Works. She was propelled under steam by a four-bladed screw, but most of her battery of eleven 8-inch rifles was located below on the gun deck in the manner of an eighteenth-century ship-of-the-line.

With her three tall masts and long bowsprit, the *Trenton* was still a handsome ship, or would have been, had her lines not been spoiled by the ugly stack amidships that belched black smoke into the clean blue air. She came into harbor just before eight o'clock in the morning, her Admiral's pennant flying and her signal flags hung high; the smoke rose almost directly aloft, for at the moment the harbor was in dead calm. As *Trenton* moved into the harbor, light airs sprang up from the west-southwest to catch the flags, a good indication of bettering weather, since danger usually came from the opposite direction.

Trenton moved in to anchor at the very edge of the harbor. All usual spaces were taken by the other six warships, eight merchantmen, and several small island traders; Apia harbor had never been so crowded as it became on that day.

As *Trenton* came in, Captain Kane in the *Calliope* ordered his gunners to fire a 13-gun salute to the American flagship. The British were followed by a salute from S.M.S. *Olga,* the German squadron leader, and as the echoes of the *Olga's* guns died down, *Trenton* returned the honor.

For the better part of the morning the ships in the harbor were wreathed in gunsmoke. The American ships, the screw sloop U.S.S. *Vandalia* and the *Kansas*-class gunboat U.S.S. *Nipsic,* also responded with salutes of gunfire to the flag; at 9:30 the men of all the American ships were mustered at general quarters and inspected by their captains; then came a round of visits, most of them to the *Trenton*, where American Rear Admiral L. A. Kimberly was receiving. American Vice Consul William Blacklock went aboard the *Trenton* accompanied by an honorific 13-gun salute. The British Consul visited the Admiral, and again the guns boomed out.

Only the German Consul General stayed away.

It was indicated then, on March 11th, that the political weather was worse than the physical, although physically the weather began to change. By ten o'clock on that morning of March 11th, the wind shifted to east-northeast; then it swept down from the northeast, the usual weather quarter, and brought more clouds and rain. From noon until three o'clock in the afternoon came a light, varying breeze that moved around the clock from northeast to southwest and then dropped completely to a dead calm that lasted for an hour. By five o'clock a drizzle cut the calm. A slight variable breeze set in, blowing from all points of the compass, and lasted until eight o'clock that evening; then the skies cleared and it became fair and cool, with a gentle breeze blowing from the south.

Faced with the problem of interpreting such weather, all the captains relied on the advice of the experienced South Sea captains ashore, and the expert verdict was already established: the stormy season was coming to an end, and there was no further danger of a typhoon.

The day following Admiral Kimberly's arrival, March 12th, was an especially pleasant day, with a fresh offshore breeze from the southwest and sunshine all day. It rained so heavily on March 13th that Admiral Kimberly sent an officer ashore to check with the local captains again, especially because the barometer began to fall. The verdict was the same: from the experience of previous years the falling barometer was perfectly normal and meant nothing more than rain.

Thursday, March 14th, was gloomy and rainy, with the

glass falling slowly, steadily, and although the seven captains and the American Admiral were confident of the judgment of their local informants, they took ordinary precautions at this point checking anchor chains, clearing boilers, and making ready for possible storm. The barometer was fluctuating; at noon the glass read 29.70; it rose a bit in the afternoon, but by midnight had dropped to 29.60. The sky was overcast and dark with scud flying along the decks and frequent squalls.

Had the ships been anchored in the fine deepwater harbor at Pago Pago on Tutuila Island, the captains would not have worried about the weather. But Apia's harbor is nothing like Pago Pago's and might not have been considered by some to be a harbor for seagoing warships at all, had it not been for the political troubles that assailed the islands.

The island of Upolu, where Apia stands, was the most important commercial district in the four isles of the archipelago, largely because of the heavy foreign investment in coconut plantations in the decade just past. There was a good market for coconut oil and copra in Europe and in Asia, and so Apia's harbor was made to do heavy service, without regard for its limitations in housing heavy ships. Yet, so low was the regard of many South Pacific seafarers for the Apia harbor that author Robert Louis Stevenson referred to it as a "so-called harbour."

The trouble was the coral. The red and white skeletons of the little polyps that make the coral had fused by the millions to cover the sides of the rocky volcanic harbor on the north side of Upolu Island. The mouth of the harbor faces almost due north. All around the north side of the island the barrier reef extends out nearly a mile past the shore, and the only reason there is any indentation that could be called a harbor is that the constant eroding action of the fresh waters from two rivers, the Mulivai and the Vaisingano, have washed away a narrow trench in the coral, leaving a small sandy beach around the mouth of the Vaisingano, but sharp reef close in to shore.

The harbor is shaped like a wide-mouthed jar, not quite three-quarters of a mile long, with an entrance three cables wide (three-tenths of a nautical mile). At no point is the harbor wider than the mouth, and the reef undulates along the sides in an irregular pattern. Under normal conditions, the seafarer would neither know nor care that the bottom of the harbor is also coral reef, kept low by the surging of the fresh water, which kills the tiny animals that make the coral, but underlaying the mud and sea vegetation into which an anchor would hold fast with a solid, hard, slippery base.

That was what Apia called a harbor, not even protected by a narrow neck to keep the surf from thundering in and out as it crossed the reef. Any warship would do well to keep away from the spiky reef altogether, and if necessity brought her into Apia, it was apparent that a captain must be on the alert at all times against the danger of bad weather. Naval discretion would dictate that at the first sign of a blow or the dropping of the glass he get up steam and put out to sea, to ride out the storm in deep water.

CHAPTER TWO

Three Allegiances

T HE FALLING BAROMETER on the night of March 14th
would have caused the Admiral and all six captains to
agree to steam out, under normal conditions. But the conditions in which the six ships found themselves this dirty
Thursday night were far from normal. Naval discretion was
not the primary consideration, or, one might say, naval
strategy called for an exercise of another kind of discretion,
particularly on the part of the American commander, Admiral Kimberly. The unpleasant situation in which German,
American, and British ships found themselves was caused by
the combination of the rivalry of three Samoan princes for
the throne of the islands and the cupidity of a handful of
assorted foreigners vying for commercial leadership in this
once happy land.

In 1881 there lived in Samoa the princes Laupepa, Tamasese, and Mataafa, each claiming that he should be made
king of all the islands. But by Samoan custom the king must
hold the allegiance of the provinces of Malietoa, Natoaitele,
Tamasoalii, Tuiaana, and Tuiatua. Laupepa could claim the
allegiance of the first three of these principalities, Tamasese

held the fourth, and Mataafa the fifth. Baring his power, Laupepa had himself crowned king on March 19, 1881. Within a month the provincial chiefs of Tuiaana and Tuia- tua met and elected Tamasese as *their* king for two years, with Mataafa to be king for the next two years.

In the year 1881 three foreign consuls lived in Samoa, an Englishman, an American, and a German named Captain Zembsch, a gentle man who was known among the Samoans as "the gentleman who acted justly." The aggressive member of the triumvirate was Consul Churchward, the Englishman.

Fortunately for the welfare of Samoa of 1881, the German commercial interests, and not the British, were paramount. German economic power had been brought to the islands by John Caesar Godeffroy, merchant of Hamburg. Godeffroy had never set foot on his empire in the Pacific, but his serv- ants had built ten thousand acres of palm forest for the production of copra, which could be taken to civilized places and squeezed for the oil so valuable in making soap and mar- garine, with a residue that made fodder. John Caesar Godef- froy had no ambitions other than commercial ones, but a few years later when he failed in business after a hopeful but unfortunate speculation in Westphalian iron, the Samoa property was taken over by a corporation, the *Deutsche Handels und Plantagen Gesellschaft für Sud-See Inseln zu Hamburg*. Since no one in Samoa but the Germans could pronounce the name, and not even a Hamburger could use it in conversation, the title was soon shortened to The Old Firm, or simply The Firm.

When the conflict began between the two kings, Laupepa and Tamasese, the three consuls met together and arranged a treaty of peace, which was imposed on Samoa by its foreign protectors. In the 1880s the power of a consul from the West- ern world was so immense as to be almost unbelievable. By a stroke of the pen he could summon a warship from his homeland, a ship carrying enough men armed with rifles to overpower the entire Samoan army, which was still equipped with spears, swords, and warclubs.

To avoid bloodshed among the Samoans, the consuls had agreed that Laupepa should be king and Tamasese should be vice-king. Mataafa was reduced to longing and hoping. Under this treaty, called the Treaty of Lackawanna, all three powers pledged themselves to this fretful system; they further agreed to respect the independence of the Samoan kingdom.

Then came 1882 and the birth of German imperialism. German properties in Samoa were valued at perhaps a million dollars that year. They included the ten thousand acres of palm trees, planted gracefully in long alleys, intersected by broad avenues up which the carts were driven for harvesting the crop, and surrounded by hedges of fragrant lime. Some seven hundred contract laborers worked these fields and forests for The Old Firm. Early on, Americans, Britons, and Germans had increased their capital by "blackbirding," or importing illegal labor from the Fijis and other islands, but this, too, had been stopped by consular fiat as unhealthy for the economy of the kingdom, and even The Old Firm had not been able to change the ruling. The Samoans declared that the black-skinned foreigners were cannibals, to a man, and The Old Firm had suffered depredations on its cattle herds, so the ruling was not too distasteful.

Yet with the ruling began a struggle among the Western elements. In 1885 the Germans forced another convention on the Samoans: the right to make laws and levy taxes was vested in a council of two Germans and two Samoans. The Samoans did not want to sign this agreement, so two German warships were brought into Apia harbor and Laupepa was informed that the ships would shortly "intervene."

King Laupepa was a conscientious, educated man. He had studied for the ministry before his path became clear, and

personally, he suffered intensely in behalf of Samoans op-
pressed by the foreigners. Without telling the foreigners,
Laupepa and Tamasese abdicated their royal positions, pub-
licly humiliated themselves by groveling before the German
consulate, and backed by forty-eight Samoan chiefs, offered
the rulership of Samoa to Great Britain.

Less than two weeks after the king had offered his memorial to Queen Victoria in November, 1885, the Germans
secured a copy of the letter and became furious. They called
in dozens of chiefs, spoke loudly of the treachery of Laupepa,
and in the end chose the dull, solemn, but ambitious
Tamasese to be new King of Samoa.

Tamasese was armed by the Germans and financed by the
Germans, and he went home to his village of Leulumoenga
and raised the flag signifying that he was king. But Laupepa
would not be deposed; since England had not accepted his
offer, he resumed the kingship and prepared to fight for it.
The Germans forced him out of Mulinuu, his capital, so
he came to Apia and raised his flag early in 1886. The Germans sent an officer and ten men from the cruiser *Albatross*
to the scene, and one sailor climbed the tree flying the flag
and brought the banner down.

The consuls of the United States and Britain watched this
ceremony, protested, and went home to write their governments. Some weeks later, official Washington took cognizance
of the dispute, and Secretary of State Bayard promised Laupepa the United States would honor its treaty of 1878, but
asked the king to do nothing in the interim.

So Samoa languished under two kingdoms and three em-
pires. Dr. Stuebel, the new German Consul, seized the town
of Apia and hoisted the German war flag. The American
Consul began flying the Stars and Stripes. For a time in 1886
war seemed to threaten. In the United States the Republicans
made Samoa a campaign issue for the Congressional elections

of 1886. President Cleveland did not wish to talk about going to war in behalf of American commercial interests in Samoa, and as for American citizens, there were fewer than fifty of them among the two hundred foreigners in Apia. The issues of tariff, worsening economic conditions, and Samoa brought the Republican opposition into control of the U.S. Senate, and in 1887 Senator Sherman and the others of the Republican majority on the Foreign Relations Committee began to make their own foreign policy, conceived in their Senate chambers and executed in the press.

However, for a year there was relative quiet, as Germany and the United States seemed to acknowledge that their consuls had gone too far. Consul Stuebel was replaced by Consul Becker, for the Kaiser, and Consul Harold Marsh Sewall, a bachelor in his twenties, came out for the United States. King Kalakaua of Hawaii created an interesting diversion—no more than that—when he attempted to create a Polynesian federation, which would include Samoa.

That spring and summer of 1887, President Cleveland and Secretary Bayard countered the Republican fulminations for imperialism in the Pacific by arranging a triparty conference, among the United States, Britain, and Germany, in Washington to resolve the Samoan issue.

Alas, the conference languished. The German Government proposed to appoint a governor representing the power with the greatest commercial interest in the islands. The other two powers would simply have the right to approve the person involved and to register their approval or disapproval every five years as a new governor was appointed. Since the "power with the greatest commercial interest" was Germany, this plan suited neither the United States nor Britain. The Americans proposed the creation of an executive council to rule the islands. It would consist of King Laupepa, Vice-King Tamasese, and representatives of each of the three big powers.

The Germans would not accept this plan, and the British did not like it, either. The conference recessed on July 26th, with mutual assurances of good will and promises by the German Government that the interests of the United States would be recognized and protected, but in spite of their expressions of good will in Washington, the Germans acted in quite a different fashion in Samoa. By mid-August, 1887, five German warships stood in Apia, the 3,000-ton *Bismarck*, the *Korvettenkreuzers Carola*, *Sophie*, and *Olga*, and the *Adler*. On August 23rd, after the regular mail ship left for Sydney, blacking out communications with the Western world for the next six weeks, Consul Becker issued an ultimatum to King Laupepa on a trumped-up charge, claiming insult to the Kaiser on his birthday.

Laupepa counseled with his chiefs and decided to stall for time. In a letter to Consul Becker he asked for four days' grace and then fled from the government building at Apia to the back country. On receiving the letter at seven o'clock that night, Consul Becker went to the government building and demanded to see Laupepa. When Laupepa did not appear, Becker seized the papers in the building and brought forth a naval force of seven hundred men with six field guns to hoist the German colors. German Marines then began a house-to-house search for Laupepa.

On August 25th, the German warships began flying the colors of Tamasese at their forepeaks, and the new king was given a royal 21-gun salute in Apia harbor and marched through the capital with a guard of honor from the ships. Consul Becker, in his consul's uniform, announced to the world and the other consuls that Germany recognized the government of Tamasese. The British and American consuls retorted that their governments still recognized Laupepa.

Two days later, German Consul Becker declared martial law in Samoa, and on September 1st the German squadron dispersed among the various islands of the Samoan group to carry the word that Tamasese was the new king. They bore proclamations signed by Tamasese and Samoan chiefs who made speeches in all the villages they could reach.

In the mountains of Upolu where he was hiding, Laupepa sent for Mataafa, the third princeling who had competed so unsuccessfully in the contest for the crown. Mataafa decided to try to mediate between the new (German) government and the old. He visited the *Bismarck* and was welcomed aboard the flagship. But once there, he was informed that there could be no peace in Samoa until Laupepa gave himself up and went into exile. The Germans proposed to take him aboard a warship and remove him from the islands. Laupepa wandered far into the mountains, and the Germans searched for him everywhere, they thought, but they did not find him. Seumanu Tafa, the high chief of Apia, had joined the king, and his warriors guarded the passes and approaches to the king's hiding place.

On September 10th, King Laupepa came down to Apia in secret to visit American Consul Sewall and ask for help. Sewall was indignant over the treatment given the king by the Germans, and by his own Government, for the State Department in Washington counseled only dally and delay. All Consul Sewall could do was assure Laupepa of his personal support and warn him to stay away from the Germans.

On September 16th, Consul Becker was tired of playing cat and mouse. He sent a letter to Laupepa, warning him that if he did not give himself up before ten o'clock the next day, Samoa would be ravaged by the Germans. Laupepa was a courageous man, and he no longer hesitated. He wrote a letter of farewell to the people of Samoa, then set out for the banks of the Vaisingano for a meeting with Mataafa. On the bank of the river he bequeathed care of Samoa to Mataafa, sure that he was going to death or permanent exile. Around

two o'clock in the afternoon, Laupepa left Mataafa and went
to the German Naval Hospital on the beach road. An hour
later, a triumphant Consul Becker led him forth and to the
wharf, where he was escorted into a small boat and taken
aboard the *Bismarck*. The next day the *Adler* took him to sea,
away from Samoa. The *Adler* put in on the coast of Australia,
and Laupepa was transferred to the *Albatross,* then taken
around the Cape of Good Hope to the Cameroons, where he
was held in exile by the German governor.

Laupepa's manner of going gave backbone to the opposition forces within Samoa, for in his final message to his
people, this is what he said:

To All Samoa

On account of my great love to my country and my great
affection to all Samoa, this is the reason that I deliver up
my body to the German government. That government may
do as they wish to me. The reason of this is, because I do
not desire that the blood of Samoa shall be spilt for me
again. But I do not know what is my offense which has
caused their anger to me and to my country.

Tuamasanga farewell. Manono and family, farewell. So
also Salfai Tutuila, Aana and Atua, farewell. If we do not
again see one another in this world, pray that we may be
again together above.

Thereafter, from the autumn of 1887 until the autumn
of 1888, the government of Samoa by the Germans and their
puppet king was virtually undisputed by Britain and the
United States. So vigorous had been Consul Sewall's dispatches home about the worsening situation that in October,
1887, the U.S. Navy steamer *Adams* was sent to Samoa on
station, but Commander Leary spent most of his time avoid-
ing the American consulate and consulting with Captain von
Widersheim of the *Adler*.

The principal opposition to the Germans came from a Mr. Moors, an American merchant in Apia, Consul Sewall, and the young American clerk, William Blacklock. Moors and Sewall both took occasion in the next few months to make trips home to Washington to lay the state of affairs before Government officials. Getting little support from the Cleveland Administration, they turned to the Republican leaders of the Senate and aired the tale of German deceit. In the Senate, tempers began to rise, and once again, in the Presidential and Congressional elections, Samoa became an issue. One reason for the excitement about Samoa in the United States was a growing feeling for imperialism; many Americans wanted to step in and place a protectorate over the islands. Another reason was the letter sent by Laupepa to Consul Sewall on the eve of the former's exile:

> When the chief Tamasese and others first moved the present troubles it was my wish to punish them and put an end to the rebellion; but I yielded to the advice of the British and American consuls. Assistance and protection was repeatedly promised to me and my government if I abstained from bringing war upon my country. Relying upon these promises, I did not put down the rebellion. Now I find that war has been made upon me by the Emperor of Germany, and Tamasese has been proclaimed King of Samoa. I desire to remind you of the promises so frequently made by your government, and trust that you will so far redeem them as to cause the lives and liberties of my chiefs and people to be respected.

Consul Sewall made excellent use of that letter in his trip home to Washington, and soon the American newspapers were filled with the story of Samoa, so that Americans were aroused over the treatment of people halfway around the world, people they would never see.

In the tensions that followed and increased, the situation

of Apia would play a major role, odd as it might be that the geography of a miserable village would have its part in the determination of world-shaking events.

Apia lies at the bottom of a tall, forested mountain and strings along the shore from Mulinuu Point to the west to Matautu on the east. Mulinuu is flat and wind-swept, and in 1888 was planted with palm trees that backed up against a swamp of mangroves. The land under the palms was occupied by the village that was the legendary home of the Samoan kings, but so far had the tentacles of German power reached that the land had passed into the hands of the Germans in the foreclosure of a debt incurred by Samoan royalty. East of Matautu lay the headquarters of The Old Firm, and east of these, on the single street, lay the village of Matafele, which had become the German community. Here were located the German consulate, the German Catholic mission, German *Bierstuben,* and German stores and German bars. Matafele ended where the Mulivai River is bridged by the road, and that bridge represented the end of the German town, with the exception of the Naval Hospital, which was located on the other side of the Mulivai. West of the river the atmosphere was Anglo-Saxon, and this was Apia proper, the town itself. Here were the stores of the Englishmen and the Americans, the Anglican church, the English mission, the English-language newspaper, *The Samoa Times and Island Advertiser,* and the American and British consulates. Then the road bridged the Vaisingano River and undulated east to Matautu Point. All this was the *Eleele Sa,* as it is called in Samoan, the Forbidden Territory—the Neutral Zone of the treaties. Apia was governed by a three-power council— the consuls plus an assessor for each consul—who appointed a governing magistrate, rotating the appointment every few months among German, American, and British subjects in the town.

In the fall of 1887 a German magistrate happened to be in office, and Consul Becker worked another of his *coups d'état,* suspending the municipal government by three powers and turning the government of Apia over to Tamasese, who in turn appointed the German magistrate as permanent judge, a violation of the treaties.

With so much control, the Germans continued to violate the treaties and, worse, to infringe on the profits of American and British businessmen in the community. The Samoans fared even more poorly, in the German effort to secure Tamasese's throne and their power. In January, 1888, the chiefs Asi, Maunga, and Tuiletufunga were deported to the Marshall Islands because they continued loyal to Laupepa. Actually, most of Samoa continued loyal to the exiled king, and Tamasese and his German friends controlled little but the north central section of Upolu, which meant Apia and its environs. They collected taxes all over the island; as soon as the German soldiers left a village, it reverted to its old ways, but they paid the taxes. There was no open opposition to the tyrants; there was no leadership for opposition. Mataafa had disclaimed his royal position as a prince and declared himself to be a private person, and he remained very quiet. The Germans were on the road to success. Then the ambitious Tamasese assumed the title *Malietoa,* which belonged to the exiled Laupepa. Only a Polynesian would know how much this action meant in a country where names have magic about them, where the common names for axe, blood, and even food have taboos, where certain words may not be spoken in the presence of a prince. The mysticism of Samoa held high the title *Malietoa;* it was Laupepa's by inheritance, and it was a total violation of custom for Tamasese to assume the name. Tamasese compounded his crime by beginning to collect *Malietoa* mats, which are like Western coats of arms.

Soon rebellion was brewing in Samoa, and by the end of

August the forest was filled with rebellious men who were collecting guns. On the night of August 31st they planned to seize Mulinuu, the seat of Samoan power. Tamasese's German adviser, a soldier of fortune named Captain Brandeis, learned of the uprising and straightaway called troops to put it down. They went out that very night to fight.

The rebels moved back to the mountains, leaving a rear guard under a young warrior named Saifaleupolu. There was a fight, several warriors fell, and Saifaleupolu was killed. The Tamasese forces came back to Apia, victorious, but the rebellion against the Germans had begun.

Five days later, the Germans decided to make an example of the little island of Manono, whose chief had joined the rebellion.

Captain Fritze had replaced Captain von Widersheim as commander of the *Adler,* and he was the one sent to do the dirty job. On the morning of September 5th, he loaded the *Adler* with Tamasese warriors and took some Samoan war canoes in tow. He steamed to Manono and shelled the island, and the landing force went ashore to burn the village. No one was there. The men were gone to war, and the women and children were hiding in the forest.

Captain Fritze did not like this task. When the American Commander Leary protested the use of a German ship to fight women and children, Fritze replied that he was under the orders of Consul Becker and had no choice. With this incident the camaraderie between the American and German vessels stopped, and from September on, the *Adams* and the *Adler* watched one another carefully, each prepared for an action that would lead to war.

Mataafa soon joined the rebels, was crowned king, and marched on Apia, 6,000 warriors adhering to his cause. They attacked Matautu and captured that point and Apia town.

The German puppet forces were then confined to the western point of Mulinuu.

Soon the war was stalemated. Mataafa controlled most of the land, but the *Adler*'s guns and men could cut them down like jackstraws. There were meetings and discussions among the representatives of the three big powers, and in October *Calliope* steamed into the harbor carrying the flag of Rear Admiral Fairfax, and a truce was arranged neutralizing Apia. It was a very sorry truce, and did not work at all; soon there was firing all around the harbor, and the lives of civilians were in danger.

Admiral Fairfax left the gunboat *Lizard* to protect British property and went off to Sydney to report to his Government. Soon the *Adler*, the *Adams*, and the *Lizard* had sent Marines ashore as armed guards at their consulates, and Apia was in a state of siege. The Americans and the English traders supplied the insurgents with guns, and the Germans supplied Tamasese's men.

This state of affairs could not continue long, for in the late hours of the night each consul was writing home to his Government. In response to the pleas of Consul Becker, the *Eber* was dispatched from the Gilbert Islands to Apia and arrived on November 22nd, although neither she nor any of the ships interfered directly with the forces on land, following the single *Adler* bombardment of September. Left alone, the Samoans fought among themselves; sniping continued all during the fall, and Mataafa attacked the Tamasese headquarters at Saluafata, west of Apia, without success.

So it was an impasse.

In the United States there were many changes during these months of tension and warfare in Samoa. President Cleveland lost his bid for reelection, and the imperialist Republicans ruled the Senate Foreign Relations Committee, with a Republican Administration due to come into office on March

4, 1889. Washington was therefore laboring with a lame-duck Government, a President whose policies had been rejected by the voters, and a Congress that would not meet until December for any business of note. Secretary Bayard ordered Consul Sewall home and discharged him as "too independent" to represent America in Samoa. It might be said that as far as action was concerned, the United States in the winter of 1888/89 was at its weakest point.

It was quite the reverse with the Germans. Since ascending the throne a few months earlier, the new Kaiser had devoted much of his time to naval and colonial affairs.

The young Emperor was twenty-nine years old when he assumed power, but he was not a thoughtful, mature man, as one might expect of someone trained for kingship. In his youth he had never been on good terms with his parents, and he ignored his responsibilities, so he had few friends. He admired Prince Otto von Bismarck, his father's Chancellor, and regarded himself as the old man's most distinguished pupil in the arts of government and empire building. Wilhelm II could scarcely have been more deluded, for all he saw were the outward trappings of Bismarck policy, not the responsible policies behind the façade. Bismarck had consolidated Germany in 1871 behind Kaiser Wilhelm I and to do so had built an autocratic, militaristic system. But the system was built for tactical reasons, and the Prince firmly intended to do away with it and seek a rapprochement with England and Russia. The Chancellor was very much concerned with social reforms, which he knew were overdue, and he wanted to increase the participation of the middle class in German affairs.

The new Kaiser came to the throne with hopes for expansion of the Empire. He dreamed of far-flung colonies and a great navy that would challenge Britannia everywhere in the seven seas. Immediately Wilhelm II took a dislike to

Bismarck's flexible foreign policy and decided that the old man was growing senile and crotchety. He laid his plans to get rid of the Chancellor, and in this late winter of 1889, Wilhelm II was working to that end. Consequently, the winds that began to strengthen in Samoan waters in the early hours of March 14th were no more confusing than the political winds that blew in Berlin.

The Kaiser was not yet ready for a confrontation with his Chancellor on domestic policies, but he was showing his independence through his personal interest in the activities of the naval forces overseas. A German navy had not really existed as late as 1876, but in 1889 it consisted of 4,100 men and 19 ships with 158 guns, not counting rapid-fire or machine guns. Most of these ships were stationed along the coast of Africa, where the German Empire had acquired three colonies. The headquarters of the German Cruiser Squadron was in East Africa. It was the Kaiser's strategy to maintain a highly mobile striking force for use anywhere in the world. Kaiser Wilhelm's preoccupation with Samoa was shown when he detached the second largest ship of his *Kreuzergeschwader*—Cruiser Squadron—to conduct the war against the Samoan kingdom.

The shadow of war hung dark and low over Samoa, as dark a spirit as the clouds that massed above the anchored fleet.

CHAPTER THREE

The Storm

D URING FOUR LONG DAYS all eyes in the harbor had been focused on the American flagship. As long as she remained in harbor, no matter how dirty the weather, none of the other ships would stir. The senior German officer, no matter what he thought of the change in the weather, could not afford to take his little fleet out of the harbor and leave it to the Americans. To lose prestige by fleeing in the face of a bit of weather was more than he could bear.

The most important German ship in the harbor was *Kreuzerkorvette Olga,* a 12-gun ship that carried a crew of 267. Like the big American men-of-war, she was a modified sailing ship, 226 feet long, three-masted, and ship-rigged to the topgallant yard. She displaced 2,169 tons, and she was rounder in the bottom, squarer in the stern, and blunter of nose than the Americans, but otherwise comparable, with engines capable of generating 2100 horsepower.

Olga's captain was *Korvettenkapitän* Freiherr von Erhardt, and although she was the largest German ship in harbor, oddly enough, under the German seniority system Captain von Erhardt was not the senior officer of the German fleet.

The captain of S.M.S. *Adler, Korvettenkapitän* Fritze, held the honor. His little ship was dwarfed by the *Olga*. She was 177 feet long, carried a crew of only 128 men, had four guns, and her engines were not a third as powerful as *Olga*'s; she could generate only 650 horsepower with all boilers at full pressure. In that respect she was neither as modern nor as safe a ship as the third German vessel in Apia, the gunboat *Eber*, for although the 575-ton *Eber* carried only 87 men, her captain, *Kapitänlieutenant* * Wallis, knew that his ship could generate 700 horsepower to speed her engines. She was fast and safe, even in these treacherous waters.

The largest ship by far was the American flagship, the *Trenton*, 253 feet long, displacing 3,900 tons and carrying 420 officers and men, including a full Navy band. The U.S.S. *Vandalia*, at 217 feet, was a much smaller, slimmer ship, displacing 2,100 tons and carrying a crew of 200 officers and men, but although the *Trenton* was higher-rated, both ships at this time were capable of only 12 knots, which would compare equally with the potential speeds of the Germans. The third American ship, the "little *Nipsic*," as she was affectionately labeled in the navy yards, was a Civil War refit, bark-rigged, displacing 1,375 tons, and she was very slow, making only 10 knots at her best. She carried a complement of 180 officers and men.

The British warship in harbor on March 15th was H.M.S. *Calliope*, 235 feet over all, displacing 2,765 tons and carrying sixteen modern breech-loading guns, plus half a dozen torpedoes for the tubes on each side of her bow. She was the most modern ship of the international fleet, only five years old, and built for long-distance cruising. She was also the fastest ship, copper-bottomed, steel and iron wood-cased, a ship of the *Comus* class. Like all the other navies in the

* At this time, the Germans used the French spelling, *Lieutenant*.

world, the Royal Navy was still loath to give up sail for steam; *Calliope* could steam under forced draft at 14.78 knots, and she could carry 320 tons of coal, but the Admiralty much preferred to have her 280-man crew sail long distances, using the enormous sail capacity of her three masts, instead of burning up precious Cardiff coal. She was bark-rigged with two light spars on the mizzen.

Little Apia harbor, less than three-quarters of a mile long and three-tenths of a mile wide at its widest point, was hard put this first March fortnight to accommodate all these men-of-war and the dozen smaller commercial vessels that rode at anchor there. It might be said that she did not accommodate them all, for *Trenton,* the last to arrive, was barely inside the wide mouth of the harbor and received no real protection from the open sea, anchored opposite a particularly vicious coral point called Cape Horn. In any event, *Trenton* could not have come in too close to the mouth of the Vaisingano River, where the coral disappeared, because the harbor was shallow for her. *Trenton* drew slightly more than twenty feet of water and certainly was not comfortable with less than ten feet under her keel. That requirement restricted her to less than half the harbor, and she was anchored in just about thirty feet at the outermost limit of the haven.

Because of the restricted space, the warships were clustered together in what was called the East Harbor, on the Matautu Point side of the bay. Naval experts had earlier listed the East Harbor as capable of anchoring four naval vessels. As for the West Harbor, it was useful only for inter-island schooners and smaller craft, since much of the water was less than twenty feet deep. Several of the merchant ships and coasters were anchored in the West Harbor, but in the East were also the 600-ton German merchantman *Peter Godeffroy* and *Santiago,* a Norwegian sailing ship of 400 tons. These lay inside the warships, protected by them.

The innermost warships were the *Adler* and the *Nipsic,* standing apart like a pair of unfriendly dogs, each watching the other, day and night, as they had been doing for many weeks. *Calliope, Olga,* and *Eber* occupied another line almost at a right angle to the sandy beach, and outside in the entrance, between the reefs, lay *Vandalia* and *Trenton,* the latecomers.

All these ships were moored according to local custom, with anchors running east and west, clear hawse to the north, and with kedges out astern to keep the ships' heads into the high swell in Apia harbor.

At midnight Lieutenant W. H. Allen of the *Trenton* took the middle watch, and although he duly noted in the log the puffing of the breezes, otherwise he indicated there was not too much difference from the weather they had been taking off and on for the past four days.

By 8 a.m. on March 15th the weather was overcast, rainy, and squally. This condition prevented the officer on the bridge from observing early the signs of a bad storm—call it typhoon, hurricane, cyclone, or *orkan.* The usual warning signs are long, feathery cirrus clouds, a thickening cirrus veil, and halos and fiery tints at sunset and dawn, which give rise to the old mariner's couplet:

> Red sky at night, sailor's delight;
> Red sky in the morning, sailor take warning.

No red sky had been seen on the evening of March 14th, not in the vicinity of Apia harbor, and there was nothing but drizzle and scud in the breeze as March 15th came adawning.

During this watch the barometer fell steadily. Aboard *Trenton* Lieutenant L. G. Reamey stopped occasionally to tap the glass, without bettering his findings. The breeze switched to south and began to stiffen, and by four bells (6 a.m.) he deemed it wise to awaken Captain N. H. Farquhar and report on the worsening weather. The Captain said to light more fires, so he sent orders to the engine room that the fires under three more boilers should be lit. Twenty minutes later, another boiler was set to heat as the wind strengthened to Force 6.

Lieutenant Reamey began to batten down for a blow. The fourth cutter had been left alongside, serving as the Admiral's barge for his frequent trips to shore in the first days of the *Trenton*'s stay in harbor. Lieutenant Reamey ordered the cutter inboard, and the boat was hoisted; then the port lower boom was brought alongside. The lower gratings of the gangways were unshipped, because the sea was beginning to lap at them and they might easily be torn loose and lost, even causing damage to the hull if they were slapped into the ship at an angle by a heavy sea. At six o'clock Lieutenant Reamey released four sailors who had been confined to the brig, as their general court-martial sentences ended, and made note that another sailor had been brought aboard by a bumboat—twenty-four hours overtime on leave. That man's conduct would be brought to the attention of the First Lieutenant in the later hours of the morning.

By 7:18 the *Trenton*'s engineering department reported that steam was firm in the boilers, and the Lieutenant could relax a little. The harbor was rough, but not so rough that the shore boats were not out, delivering to the mixed fleet foodstuffs from the warehouses in Apia. That morning the *Trenton* took on 316 pounds of meat, 316 pounds of vegetables, and 253 pounds of bread.

The barometer fell .14 inch during this watch, to 29.42, and the change in the weather was apparent to every seagoing man aboard every ship in the harbor. The other ships were doing much the same that *Trenton* did: getting up steam but not pressing it, so as to save coal, bringing in boats, belaying loose lines, making sure the cross was in the hawse, for the anchors were beginning to feel the strain of the sea. The *Calliope* had started fires in three boilers at 4:30. The Germans lit their fires and took on provisions.

When Lieutenant Richard Scott took the watch of the *Trenton* at eight o'clock in the morning, the breeze was light to very fresh, and squalls kept sweeping in from the south-southeast for the first two hours of the watch. The overcast continued, and as the squalls diminished, the drizzle increased. The barometer continued to fall, and just before noon it reached 29.30, a fall of another .12 inch in four hours. Captain Norman Farquhar conferred with Admiral Kimberly. They were in for a storm, they now knew.

The harbor was too rough to be going ashore to check weather again with the old skippers and local experts. The decision Admiral Kimberly had to make, for the third time, was whether to ride out the storm in harbor or hoist anchor and head for the open sea.

The Admiral reviewed his instructions. He had been ordered to Samoa from San Francisco to give full protection and defense to United States citizens and United States property which was said to be threatened by the German war effort and declaration of martial law in Samoa. He had been told to consult with the United States Consul, and he had done so. He had been ordered to examine the archives and collect information as to the military and political situations, and as far as he had been able in four days, he had carried out that part of his task, as well. He had also been ordered to protect the native government of Samoa "against subjugation and displacement" by Germany "in violation of positive agreement and understanding between the treaty powers."

This last part of the Admiral's instructions now gave him

pause. He had been told in the same telegram that carried his orders that the German Government had invited the American Government to join in establishing order in Samoa, but *order* was not quite the same as *independence,* and the Admiral's orders were to secure the independence of the Samoan kingdom. Further, the insult offered him and the American Government on his arrival by Consul Knappe did not augur well for cooperation. The Admiral had been informed, also, that the Samoans who were fighting the Germans were simply awaiting his arrival and expected that under the aegis of the United States all their problems would be solved.

These considerations in mind, the Admiral looked up at the threatening sky and out at the dirty gray waves rolling in from the open sea, and he affirmed his previous decisions to ride out the storm in harbor. The local pilots and old residents had assured him that the backbone of the year's weather was broken; he did not believe them now, but he did not particularly care. With steam up, with four heavy anchors, with top-hamper down, he expected no serious trouble with the ships. All the better if the lighter German ships felt impelled to cut and run before the weather. *Trenton* would stay, and so would *Vandalia* and *Nipsic.* American prestige must be maintained, and it would be.

Had Admiral Kimberly been privileged to have at hand the modern meteorological devices of the twentieth century he might have changed his mind, but probably he would not have. There was no evidence at all of dirty weather at Suvaroff Island, the usual beginning of the Samoa weather chain, and the American schooner *Equator* had experienced nothing worse than thick, squally weather at noon on March 14th at 12° S., 170° 50′ W. The storm that was heading for Samoa had originated as a relatively light blow some three hundred miles northeast of the islands on March 13th and had passed right over the *Equator* without hurting her, indicating very little severity.

The only thing that might have changed the Admiral's mind was something he was not now even considering. Had he made another visit ashore on the morning of March 15th, he would have found the oldest inhabitants of Apia singing a new tune. Before eight o'clock in the morning the barometer had hit a new low for the Samoan Islands; in the terrible death-dealing storm of 1882 the glass had fallen to 29.45, and by noon on this March 15th it was below 29.30 and still dropping.

CHAPTER FOUR

The Men-of-War

J UST BEFORE NOON Admiral Kimberly moved. He called in Captain Farquhar and told him to prepare to house the topmasts and send down the lower yards. A few moments later a signalman was detailed to pass the word to *Vandalia* and *Nipsic* to do the same and thereafter to follow the motions of the flagship. In case the weather worsened and signaling became impossible, the Admiral wanted his fleet on the alert, ready to slip chains and head for the open sea.

The Admiral was a sensitive and a sensible man. His position was difficult—this bad blow coming up before he had a real chance to get his feet on the ground. The same quality that led him to devote his spare hours to sketching and painting in water colors led him to sense that the American presence was essential to the success of his mission and that nothing must be allowed to interrupt that presence. There was the sensitive artist, grasping in fewer than half a dozen land meetings the essence of the complex political situation and acting instinctively.

But the Admiral was also a hard-bitten career officer, trained at the Naval Academy and further schooled in the rigorous life of the sailing-ship Navy, then baptized in fire in the Civil War. He was brave, cool, and competent, and he had shown it. In 1852 he had been appointed Passed Midshipman, a commission scarcely higher than that of cadet. Twelve years later he was executive officer of the steam sloop *Hartford*, the flagship of Admiral Farragut's fleet, at the battle of Mobile Bay. Now he was commander-in-chief of the Pacific Station, a responsible post that was not achieved by an officer because he possessed the sensitivity of an artist. The Admiral had plenty of solid common sense, and the willingness to plan alternative courses of action at all times. He was determined to stay in Apia harbor as long as nature let him, but if it became necessary, he wanted to be able to move—fast.

Norman H. Farquhar, the Admiral's senior captain, quite agreed with the Admiral's position, and it would not have mattered to him if he had disagreed, for he would have obeyed without question. Captain Farquhar was a cheerful, conscientious officer, and a brilliant one. He had graduated high in his class at Annapolis late in the 1850s and had been detailed as a midshipman aboard the frigate *Constellation* when she was on duty off the African coast, helping suppress the slave trade.

In the course of this duty Midshipman Farquhar distinguished himself as senior midshipman aboard. One day he was ordered to take a prize crew and sail a captured American slaver back to the United States, so with a dozen men he sailed from the Guinea coast, heading for America. A few days out, the crew was stricken with yellow fever, and the men began dropping. By the time Midshipman Farquhar reached the Virginia Capes on his way to Norfolk, he had only two men capable of standing duty, but he sailed the ship into port, anchored her, and reported for duty, as if he had done nothing remarkable.

Farquhar was promoted to lieutenant, and during the Civil War he successfully assaulted one of the island forts held by the Confederates. (The visor of his cap was torn away by grapeshot in that affair.)

After the war Captain Farquhar alternated between sea and shore duty, and his last command before the *Trenton* was as commandant of cadets at the Naval Academy at Annapolis.

Captain Farquhar had only one caveat in this crisis: in the back of his mind was a nagging worry about the *Trenton*'s major weakness as a ship. Her hawseholes, the brassbound ports through which the anchor chain and docking hawsers passed, did not lead into the upper deck or into any well deck where proper scupperage could be assured. Instead, the designers of the *Trenton* had placed her hawse-pipes so they opened into the lower berth deck forward, and in heavy weather the deck was soon sloshing in several inches of water that could only be cleared out with bucket and mop.

At noon General Signal 3917 was received aboard the *Vandalia,* and Captain C. M. Schoonmaker gave the orders to begin stripping the rig for weather. Captain Schoonmaker was another Regular Navy man, also a graduate of the Academy at Annapolis, who had just passed his fiftieth birthday while at sea. Of those years he could count thirty-five spent in the service of his Government. Schoonmaker had served with distinction in the Civil War, then on the South American Station aboard the steamer *Juniata,* and for two years in the Asiatic Squadron aboard the *Piscataqua.* He was thoroughly familiar with Pacific weather and with the ships of this little squadron, for he had been aboard the *Nipsic* in 1881 as a lieutenant commander, when she was a part of a goodwill fleet led by the *Trenton* to Europe. The Captain was not a large man, just five feet, eight inches in height, but very muscular. He prided himself on his good condition and on the condition of his ship and men. There was a problem, however, aboard all the American ships. The Admiral was an easygoing man when he had the opportunity to be, and he had granted general shore leave on arrival in Apia harbor. The men had gone ashore and had met up with the local rum, which created some difficulty for the Marine guard. Worse, the men had come back carrying fever and dysentery, and at least double the usual contingent of *Vandalia* was in sickbay, with several dozen other sailors on their feet but woozy. The same condition applied to all the American ships.

The flagship's signal was also received aboard the *Nipsic* by Commander D. W. Mullan. He was the youngest ship's commander of the group, an Annapolis man, too, in his middle forties, with thick straight brown hair, receding a bit above the forehead, and a luxurious beard and heavy mustache that completely dominated his face. Commander Mullan could by now call himself a Samoa hand, for he had brought the *Nipsic* and her present crew around the Horn and to Samoa in the fall of '88 to relieve the U.S.S. *Adams* and take duty as station ship at Apia. Mullan had arrived in the autumn, just after the Germans had run up their flag and "taken possession" of Samoa. In this difficult situation, Commander Mullan had already shown himself an able sailor-diplomat. Every day since November had carried its invitation to open violence against the Germans, and Mullan had restrained his crew and kept America out of war in the face of innumerable provocations.

Little *Nipsic* was least capable of all the American ships of riding out a blow in the harbor, and Commander Mullan knew this very well, yet he did not wince. Men went aloft within minutes to begin work on the topmasts and to drop the yards. For the work ahead *Nipsic* had but one saving grace—she drew only 11 feet 6 inches of water, and this shallow draft gave her more room for maneuver in the wash-basin harbor than any other American ship had.

In the second line of anchored warships, H.M.S. *Calliope*'s lookout spotted the activity on the *Trenton* as soon as it began and reported to the bridge that the Americans were striking lower yards and topmasts. Lieutenant Robert McAlpine, the ship's First Lieutenant, carried the word to Captain Kane, and that officer, then, was faced with the decision that had so troubled Admiral Kimberly for hours. With Captain Kane, it was not so much a question of prestige, for Britain's prestige with the Samoans would not be destroyed by *Calliope*'s absence from the harbor; the Samoan warriors owed too much to Her Majesty. But no captain wants to be the first of an international fleet to run before weather; that was simply a matter of human nature. Captain Kane's decision—to stay with the Americans—was also backed by personal experience. *Calliope* had been posted as one of a dozen ships of the British China Squadron in 1888 and had spent the Christmas holidays at Sydney because she needed dry-docking for some minor repairs after a long cruise. On December 27th Captain Kane had taken the ship to Auckland to join the squadron, and there he had been dispatched by Rear Admiral Henry Fairfax to Samoa to represent British interests and relieve H.M.S. *Royalist* on that station.

On February 2nd *Calliope* had arrived at Apia and had been there ever since, going out of harbor only once—to carry out quarterly firing as prescribed by Admiralty regulations—and then she had returned to port the same evening.

Captain Kane and the men of the *Calliope* had lived through three previous gales in this harbor and knew how to take them. On February 10th the Captain had sent a cutter out in very heavy weather to tow the trading schooner *Matauta* clear of the warship's bows, when the schooner's anchors failed to hold. The cutter crew had done so with dispatch, only to see the *Matauta* slip away later in the night and be thrown high and dry on the reef. In the gale of February 13/14, when the American barkentine *Constitution* was lost and an island schooner named *Tamasese* went down, *Calliope* had stood firm to her anchors. Captain Kane had kept steam available and brought down lower yards and topmasts then, too, but he had never had to use his engines in these storms; his anchors did the job. The Captain had great respect for those anchors, four of them, each weighing 60 cwts, iron-stocked, and fitted with a band on the shank for stowing with one davit. They were good solid, heavy anchors, and the proof of them was that while the *Nipsic* and the German warships had been forced to use their engines to ease the strain in the February blows, *Calliope* had ridden comfortably enough with anchors alone.

Aboard S.M.S. *Adler,* senior vessel of the German fleet, the first officer, *Kapitänlieutenant* von Arend, noted the activity on the *Trenton* and brought the word of the American Admiral's decision to *Korvettenkapitän* Fritze just after noon. There was considerably less enthusiasm aboard the German vessels for the prospect of remaining in port, for none of the German ships was properly equipped to resist heavy weather, as had been proved in the earlier storms. Yet a loyal officer of His Majesty, Captain Fritze, could not dream of hustling out of harbor and leaving the Americans in possession. He had ordered steam in four boilers on the middle watch, and Captains von Erhardt in *Olga* and Wallis in *Eber* had also raised steam. Now the problem for the Germans was to bring all men back aboard ship. Since they considered Samoa to be theirs, the German commanders had been quite lenient in granting shore leave to all ranks. A large contingent of German *matrossen,* then, were ashore in the beerhalls of the German section of Apia when at high noon they heard the

Adler's cannon firing signal guns in the harbor. It was the
call for all the Germans to return to their ships immediately.
Really, *Eber* should at this point have been detached and
sent to sea, for her screw had been bent in the storm of February 13/14, and with the Americans arriving in force there
had been no chance to send her away for repairs. For that
matter, the only nearby place where repairs could be made
were the British navy yards at Auckland or at Sydney, and
with the political situation as it stood, the Germans were in
no position to be asking favors from the British. Nor would
the stiff-necked Kaiser Wilhelm II countenance one of his
ships retreating in the face of a potential enemy. So the
unhappy *Eber*'s lot was to stay on, crippled, and ride out
the storm with the others.

CHAPTER FIVE

The Hiatus

A<small>T NOON</small> on March 15th, as the barometer dropped and the skies blackened, the opening of the *Adler*'s gunports to order the return of the German crews to ship recalled another day, exactly four months earlier, when the opening of those ports had nearly begun a war.

On November 14, 1888, German Consul Knappe announced disdainfully to his fellow consuls that on the following morning he would direct Captain Fritze to bombard the Mataafa camp at Laulii a few miles west of Apia. The British Consul had informed Knappe that the plantation at Laulii was British property, and that if the *Adler* attempted to destroy British property, the *Lizard* would see that she did not.

So at sunrise on the morning of November 15th, the *Adler* steamed out of Apia harbor on her warlike mission with Consul Knappe aboard. The *Lizard* came right behind her with British Consul de Coetlogon aboard, and the *Adams* was third in line, with American Consul Blacklock aboard. Blacklock had made no threats. He, having succeeded Consul Seward, was too new in his job, and he had no support from President Cleveland's State Department, but he and Commander Leary were determined that the Germans should not interfere.

The little fleet steamed west along the north shore of the island till they reached Laulii; then the *Adler* swung slightly inshore. The others followed, watchfully. The *Adler* opened her gunports. So did the *Lizard,* and so did the *Adams.*

Captain Fritze's calm good sense prevailed that day over the shouts of his consul. He did not fire, and for the moment war was averted.

On the day after that incident, the three consuls met for the first time in months and discussed their differences. They came to no conclusion, but at least they had talked instead of fighting.

The next few days of November, 1888, marked what was known in Samoa as The War of Flags. British, American, and German consuls raised flags above territory that their nationals claimed, a warning that this land must not be touched. Then one day, under German inspiration, an American flag was torn from its moorings, trampled, and partially burned. Consul Blacklock sent the mutilated remains back to Washington as evidence of the insults being offered the American nation in Samoa.

The dishonored flag arrived in Washington at about the time that the 50th Congress assembled for its last session. In the next Congress, which would take office on March 4, 1889, the Republicans would control both houses. Consequently, the statements of Chairman John Sherman of the Senate Foreign Relations Committee were heard with more respect than ever in this December. Former Consul Sewall was in Washington at this time, and he placed himself at the disposal of the Republican majority of the committee, testifying at length on the Samoan question. His testimony was widely reported in the American newspapers, and American tempers rose.

The New York World sent a war correspondent named John Klein to Samoa to live with the Mataafa army in the field.

In Samoa, tempers were rising, too. On December 11, the British ship *Richmond* brought in a cargo of kegs that were delivered to Mataafa. So insecure was the greatest of secrets in Samoa that within twenty-four hours all Apia knew that the kegs had not contained salt beef, as labeled, but 28,000 cartridges for Mataafa's guns. On December 14th, Captain von Erhardt arrived with the *Olga,* making three German ships in the harbor, with nearly five hundred men to enforce German policy.

The forces of Mataafa had occupied much of the German Vailele plantation behind Apia, and this presence was a constant annoyance to the Germans. One night a horse was stolen from the German consulate. Another night there was a riot between natives and the sailors of the *Olga.*

On December 16th, with his new ammunition Mataafa tried to land in Saluafata Bay, near the headquarters of Tamasese, to attack. Since Tamasese was occupying German land, this represented war—at least to Consul Knappe.

On December 17th the Germans decided to act—or Consul Knappe did—and Captain Fritze was under his orders. The Consul ordered Fritze to disarm Mataafa.

Captain Fritze objected to the order, but he was overruled, and Knappe's plan was put into effect. At two o'clock on the morning of December 18th a landing party left the *Olga,* fifty men in two boats under *Kapitänlieutenant* Jaeckel and Lieutenant Sieger, each man with forty rounds of ammunition, a canteen, and a day's rations.

These boats escorted a large pram which was filled with ninety sailors, fully armed and carrying the same rations, led by Lieutenants Spengler and Burchard. The Germans were to land at four o'clock to attack Vailele, which was about a mile and a half east of Apia on a small point behind the reef. Lieutenant Spengler in the pram would land on the west side of the little point Fangali. *Kapitänlieutenant* Jaeckel would lead the two boats outside the reef and land at Sunga on the east shoulder of the point. The forces would converge and trap Mataafa neatly between them. Later in the day, a war party was to leave the *Eber,* move to the Letongo mountains to disarm any Mataafa people there, and then link up with the men of the *Olga.*

The surprise might have worked, could secrets be kept in Samoa, but Tamasese's supporters must boast that on the next day they would have the heads of their enemies, and so it was known that the Germans were about to take military action.

Mataafa's men were on the alert, and spies followed the progress of the German boats as they put out of the harbor early in the morning.

Correspondent John Klein was with the Mataafa force led by Apia Chief Seumanu Tafa near the Fangali landing place where the pram would come in. In the fashion of war correspondents in those days he wore full field kit, including a revolver, which he had been known to fire in the direction of the Tamasese camp. As the pram moved in toward shore, by the light of the moon, the Samoans hailed her, and when no one responded to the hail, Klein stood up revolver in hand and hailed in English.

"Do not try to land here," he cried. "If you do, your blood will be upon your head."

Whereupon the alarm was sounded both in camp and aboard the pram. Quickly the men of the pram landed, and as quickly the Samoans called for reinforcements. It was dark, but the German sailors in their white suits made a good target. The Samoans opened fire and killed one German sailor, although the rest managed to get ashore under cover of the brush.

On the other side of the point, the two German boats landed and were also brought under fire, but the Germans managed to turn over their boats and use them as cover. Soon they captured the Vailele plantation house (which was undefended) and made it their headquarters.

Lieutenant Spengler and his ninety men from the pram moved inland, only to be surrounded by the Samoans, who were firing wildly and shouting even more wildly. The Lieutenant learned from a civilian that his compatriots had taken the plantation house, and in a series of three charges he led his men to join with *Kapitänlieutenant* Jaeckel's force there, leaving four men dead behind him.

Inside the compound, the Germans were all together, but they were surrounded on three sides, with the sea at their backs. On the left, the Samoans had cover in the long white plantation office building. In front, the Samoans were entrenched behind the long crest of the horse pasture, which commanded an excellent view of the house and garden. On the right, the Samoans were protected by a thick hedge.

Lieutenant Sieger had been seriously wounded in the fight from the boats to reach the house, and he was laid down gently on the bed of the plantation manager. For a few minutes there was relative quiet, broken by a few Samoan shouts and stray shots. Then the volleys began, with the Samoans shooting at all apertures of the house.

Their fire was wasteful, but it was also effective. In one of the first volleys Lieutenant Sieger was wounded again, this time mortally, and a few minutes later he died.

Within an hour, in the full light of day, the Samoan reinforcements began coming up, and soon they outnumbered the Germans, perhaps ten to one. With such numbers, the

Samoans began infiltrating the horse pasture toward the house, threatening the garden and the house itself. The Germans counterattacked, throwing open the doors of the house and rushing forth. They drove the Samoans from the garden, but as soon as they moved into the horse pasture, the Mataafa men began to surround them on three sides, and they were forced to retreat. The Germans came back, close to the hedge on the right, and here with his sword *Kapitänlieutenant* Jaeckel dispatched a Samoan sharpshooter who was sniping at his men.

Another hour went by, with the Samoans creeping forward again, through the pasture, and around the hedge. Another German counterattack was launched, the *matrossen* leaping forward, bayonets fixed, shouting "Hurray!" as they drove the Samoans back once again. An hour later came a third sortie, to keep the Samoans from overrunning the house.

These charges were expensive. Many white uniforms were stained with ragged splashes of red and rust, and the German ammunition supply was dwindling rapidly. Part of the cartridge boxes had been ruined in the upsetting of the boats for defense on the shore. The boxes of the dead and wounded were assembled and brought into use, but by 7:30 in the morning *Kapitänlieutenant* Jaeckel was seriously worried about their ability to withstand a frontal attack, which might come at any time. Lieutenant Spengler was wounded, so was Lieutenant Burchard, and so were forty sailors, with another thirteen who would never fight again.

The fighting had continued steadily for more than three hours, and Jaeckel was not sure that he could hold out for another hour, when the fortunes of war switched.

The *Eber* had steamed out of Apia early in the morning, before dawn, to land a force near Saluafata, and on the way back to port Captain Wallis observed the action at the plantation. From Apia came the *Adler,* as quickly as Captain Fritze could raise steam, after the word of the plight of the landing party reached him overland. At eight o'clock the *Eber* began lobbing shells into the Samoan camp, and soon the *Adler* joined her with her four guns. Captain Wallis sent a landing party ashore in the *Eber*'s longboat to rescue the besieged Germans. The party was led by *Oberbootsmannsmaat* Eberhard Krause, a tough thirty-year-old professional navy man who wore the golden earring of a sailor who had taken a sailing ship around Cape Horn in a storm. *Oberbootsmannsmaat* Krause was armed with rifle, pistol, and a dirk, and his men carried rifles and daggers, too.

Under cover of the fire of the warships they rowed swiftly in to shore. They were unobserved. The Samoan attackers were confused by the shelling. The *Eber* was shelling the Mataafa village of Letongo, and one shell killed five men sitting by a cooking pot. *Adler* was throwing her shells farther west, around the house and on the edges of the native village. In fifteen minutes *Oberbootsmannsmaat* Krause stood inside the plantation house, shaking the hand of a grateful *Kapitän-lieutenant* Jaeckel.

Here was the war that all had been dreading, not the struggle between Samoans, but the involvement of German troops in force against Mataafa, who represented to Britain and America the legitimate Government of the island kingdom.

Consul Knappe heard the news of the battle and decided that Germany must use all its force in Samoa to win the war. The *Nipsic* had now replaced the *Adams* as the American picket ship, and Commander Mullan protested to Captain Fritze, but to no avail.

Consul Knappe, in the mistaken belief that Correspondent Klein was of German birth, charged that Klein had led the attack on the Germans and demanded the correspondent's arrest and trial by court-martial. Klein had to be hidden from the Germans in the American consulate, and to be carried stealthily off the island in the *Nipsic* to escape with his life. Naturally, Correspondent Klein wrote the entire story of his experiences, and it was printed boldly by *The World* and other newspapers, arousing more Americans to fury.

On January 15, 1889, the steamer *Richmond* returned to Apia harbor, and the Germans, remembering her last cargo, boarded her, searched her, and kept possession overnight. The next day Consul Knappe formally declared war on Samoa and proclaimed martial law.

On January 20th an English traveler, Mansfield Gallien, bored with the *Richmond*'s enforced stay in Apia harbor, decided to pay a visit to Mataafa, in his camp east of Apia. Like many an English tourist of the nineteenth century, Gallien was an adventurous man and gave no thought to personal danger. He simply wanted to find out what all the shooting was about, so he went to the source.

Mataafa greeted traveler Gallien gravely and courteously, and the two talked at length. In the usual English spirit of independence Gallien suggested that Mataafa appeal to London for assistance. They had a pleasant day together, and Gallien went back to the *Richmond*.

Early on the morning of January 21st, tourist Gallien was hauled rudely from his berth by German sailors and forced to accompany them aboard the *Adler,* where he was questioned about trafficking with Germany's enemy. The arrest was carried out by the direct orders of Consul Knappe. When Captain Fritze of the *Adler* discovered what had been done, he was both angry and worried. Without consulting Knappe he sent a message on its way to Berlin.

"Is arrest of foreigners on foreign vessels legal?" he asked.

While waiting for an answer, which would take two weeks or more, Captain Fritze concerned himself with what was to be done about his civilian prisoner.

Captain Hand, commander of the British gunboat *Royalist,* solved that problem for Captain Fritze. Captain Hand came aboard the *Adler* the next day for conversation.

"I wish you would set that man ashore," he said, indicating citizen Gallien, "to save me the trouble."

Captain Fritze was only too eager to be rid of a prisoner he did not want and freed the civilian at that moment.

As Consul Knappe kept taking the law into his own hands, Captain Fritze became more distressed and let it be known that he disagreed with the policies laid down. On January 22nd Knappe suppressed *The Samoa Times and South Sea Advertiser,* because it had been critical of his conduct. Editor Cusack had already been deprived of the legal advertising of the government; now he was closed down altogether and must return full-time to his trade of carpentering.

Captain Fritze became so concerned with the course of events that he wrote to Berlin again, and soon it was known in the German colony that the two officials were at odds. The Germans sided entirely with Knappe. He was hailed and wined and dined nightly. Captain Fritze was ostracized by the German community.

Through Consul Knappe's incompetence, eagerness, or Teutonic authoritarianism—depending on the point of view —Germany had been brought to the brink of war with Britain and the United States, and if those countries insisted on honoring the letter of their treaties with Samoa, world war would result.

The news of the occurrences of December, and particularly of the burning of the American flag, brought so much pressure to bear in Washington that the Cleveland Administration was forced to act, and Admiral Kimberly, commander of the Pacific Squadron, was ordered to Samoa to enforce the American-Samoan treaty and specifically to prevent "extreme measures against the natives of Samoa."

The Admiral was in San Francisco when the word reached him in January, and he lost no time. The *Vandalia* was in San Francisco, and she was dispatched from there. He boarded the dispatch boat *Dolphin* and steamed for Panama, where his two-star flag was run up on the *Trenton*, and she set out for Samoa. The *Dolphin* was to come along a few days later.

In Berlin, when Chancellor Bismarck received reports of Consul Knappe's actions, he was furious and worried. He wasted no time in assuring the British Foreign Office and the American State Department of Germany's peaceful intentions, and he sent Knappe a sharp reprimand for his behavior. But Bismarck's star was setting; Knappe had been carrying out Kaiser Wilhelm II's policy; and within a year Bismarck would be dismissed as Chancellor. The old Chancellor's assurances were received with suspicion and misgiving in Washington, particularly by the Senate Foreign Relations Committee. An appropriation of $100,000 was voted to build and fortify a coaling station at Pago Pago, and the warhawks among the Republicans clamored for direct military action against Germany.

While Admiral Kimberly was sailing and steaming across the Pacific, the Germans were backing down slightly. At the end of February, Consul Knappe canceled his proclamation of martial law, but he did not tell Consul Blacklock that much. Instead, Captain Fritze informed Captain Schoonmaker of the *Vandalia* of this fact. At the same time, it was learned that reinforcements were being sent in strength from Bremerhaven to Apia.

The German policy had always been to lead from strength, to talk of peace and cooperation, but to continue, nevertheless, to take over control of all Upolu.

On March 3rd, Blacklock noted that the *Richmond* was again in port and again under German guard, and that four more German warships were on their way to Samoa. The news depressed him, for he expected that on arrival of the reinforcements the Germans would launch a decisive offensive against Mataafa.

"The S.S. *Lubeck* arrives from Sydney," he wrote, "and Mr. Parker, one of the editors of the *Sydney Morning Herald* arrives and is astonished to find me here, as the Germans reported to him that I had been forced to leave the country. He finds the existing state of affairs in Samoa altogether different to what he had been led to believe from German reports. . . ."

On March 3rd, from the major German naval base at Kiel had come a rumor of an engagement between an unnamed American man-of-war and *Olga*. The Americans fired first, said the German naval source. The rumor was carried across the Atlantic cable and was printed on the front pages of American newspapers on March 4th, along with speculative articles from Berlin, London, and Washington, and a reminder that a new conference on the Samoan question was scheduled to begin in Berlin sometime that same month.

The rumor was denied by official sources everywhere, but the newspapers made up for it by printing the specifications of the various ships both nations had sent to Apia, including their weaponry.

Such rumors, reports, and speculations were rife everywhere in the civilized world, and the reason for them was the communications gap. No underwater cable existed to serve the tiny Samoan archipelago. Wireless telegraphy would not become available for nearly a quarter of a century. Communication between Samoa and the outside world was carried on by way of Auckland, New Zealand, *by ship*. Regular mail and supply ships came from Auckland, and sometimes from Sydney. From these outposts of civilization there was cable contact with Europe and America via the

Australian cable system, but any news from Samoa was a good ten days in transmission to the United States.

So when Secretary of State Bayard was questioned by newspaper correspondents about the rumors, he could only say that he had not heard anything of the incident, that he doubted it had occurred, and that the reporters should be calm and remember that the United States, Britain, and Germany had "an understanding" that belligerent action in Samoa would be suspended until after the Berlin conference. The rumors persisted. In Washington, naval officers speculated that if there had been a sea battle, it was between the *Olga* and the gunboat *Nipsic*. Officially, the Navy pooh-poohed the rumor, but unofficially, high-ranking officers indicated it was quite possible there had been a fight. If the Germans had so much as fired a warning shot across the bows of the *Nipsic*, one officer said privately, it was quite probable that the gunboat had replied with a broadside.

The New York Times professed to recall the days of the *Adams* in Apia harbor and how she was "compelled to keep her decks 'cleared for action' and her position so selected as to enable her to keep a gun constantly trained on the Germans."

If the *Trenton* had been on hand and there had been reason for a fight, said *The Times*, "Captain Farquhar would have thrown the big ship's rifles into action in a twinkling."

As of March 4, 1889, the war fever was rising in Washington, for a reason that is readily understandable. On that day Grover Cleveland stepped down, and Benjamin Harrison stepped up to the Presidency of the United States. The Republican warhawks in the Senate made preparations to face Germany down. They did not really understand Grover Cleveland's forbearance in the past. Cleveland had sent a strong message to Congress in January, and this message had been the signal for the Senate's moves to fortify Pago Pago and strengthen the American Navy. Cleveland had also authorized the dispatch of Admiral Kimberly and his little fleet to Apia.

What the warhawks did not know was that Cleveland had barely been dissuaded from sending a second message to Congress on Samoa, charging that the Germans were trying to subvert the Government of Samoa for their own purposes. After March 4th, the Republican majority in Congress did not care what Cleveland had said or done. They were ripe for military action.

On March 8th in Germany the *Schlesische Zeitung* embroidered the "sinking" story. The *Olga* had been bombarding a Samoan camp, the newspaper reported, when the American ship came up to protest. The *Olga* ignored the protest, whereupon the American opened fire, sending a shell between decks and doing much damage. The *Olga* then torpedoed the American ship, which sank with all hands.

Because of the communications gap, any rumor was possible. In San Francisco, much credence was given to the report, because the Marine Quartermaster there verified the fact that the *Olga* was equipped with torpedoes. And the gap itself was illustrated by an attempt to fill it: the steamer *Alameda* had left San Francisco for Australia on February 9th, it had touched at Tutuila in the Samoan group on February 25th, and had arrived in Auckland on March 3rd. Had any engagement occurred at Apia, the news *probably* would have reached Tutuila, where the *Alameda* would have had the word and carried it to Auckland. From Auckland the report would have been *cabled* to London and then would have reached the United States.

At this point, the San Francisco papers reported, the next news from Samoa would come in on the steamship *Zealandia,* which would dock at San Francisco on March 16th, bearing news of the islands as of March 2nd.

That report was made on March 8th. The next day a report reached San Francisco apparently verifying the battle, naming the sunken American ship as the *Nipsic,* and purportedly explaining the failure of the *Alameda* to report. She had been seized by the Germans, said the story. Furthermore, the Secretary of the Navy was supposed to have telegraphed the Mare Island Navy Yard, ordering the modern steel cruiser *Charleston* to Samoa.

Hundreds of people surrounded the San Francisco newspaper offices on Market Street, waiting for every bulletin and rumor. All day long the newspapers tried to satisfy the public curiosity by issuing extras, each edition embroidering the story more than the last. The more the rumors were denied, the more they persisted, and millions of Americans were certain that war with Germany was at hand.

In the vacuum, all that the newspapers did kept the rumors alive. Noting sagely that when governments receive no news, the people are inclined to turn to any private sources, on March 9th *The New York Times* speculated on the fate of the *Nipsic*. Probably she was not sunk, said the editorial, but then again she might be, since the *Olga* boasted a battery of high-power breech-loading Krupp rifles. "Hence she could choose her distance and riddle the *Nipsic*."

If that comment was hardly the type to dispel anxiety, it did truly represent the attitude of Americans, half fearing, half welcoming the idea of conflict with Germany.

The Times published a letter from Commander Mullan of the *Nipsic*. "I hear by way of Auckland that we will have more ships here," wrote the Commander. "God knows how this affair will end."

On March 11th, the day that Admiral Kimberly arrived in Apia harbor aboard the *Trenton,* the rumors reached new heights, and even flat denials from Cabinet officers did not quell them, nor could anything end the war fever that was creeping through America except a comprehensive report, assuring the nation that the Germans had backed down from their arrogant position of power in Samoa.

American newspapers that day published a London dispatch quoting Robert Louis Stevenson, who was living in Hawaii.

"Who is Knappe?" Stevenson said. "By what process has he become the Bismarck of the Polynesian islands? What spell has been cast over the cabinets at Washington and London that Blacklock has been so long unsupported and Coetlogon has been compelled to bow his head under a public buffet?"

The strongest statement of all came from Admiral Porter of the U.S. Navy, as reported in the Washington *Evening Star,* of March 13th; Porter called for war with Germany. "We are weak on the ocean now," said the Admiral, "but there is a plan which will meet the emergency—namely, to cripple Germany while we were getting ready." He called for a Congressional appropriation of $50,000,000 to rebuild the American Navy. With that money, the Admiral said, in sixty days he could set an improved fleet "to the work of destroying German commerce."

On March 15th the editors of *The New York World* and other newspapers that advocated strong action were planning new stories on the Samoan crisis, while basically anti-war newspapers like *The New York Times* were assuring readers editorially as heartily as they could that war had not yet broken out.

As for the real state of events in Samoa, the communications gap left the world quite unaware of the drama that was beginning.

When Admiral Kimberly had arrived, after fifty-eight days at sea, and called on the American Consul, the Admiral was astounded to learn that Blacklock had not received any instructions from the Government about cooperating with his naval mission. Secretary Bayard, running true to form, had tried to keep matters as fluid as possible, by doing nothing at all.

Following his arrival in Apia on March 11th, the Admiral completed the exhausting task of rendering and accepting formal courtesies, and the next day he came ashore to consult with Consul Blacklock. While the Admiral was ashore, German Consul Knappe seized the opportunity to pay his "courtesy call" on the absent Admiral's flagship. Knappe had done the same thing a few months earlier when British Admiral Fairfax in H.M.S. *Royalist* had visited Apia. It was a veiled insult to the Admiral and to the United States, but not the kind of insult of which one could make much. Admiral Kimberly came ashore again on March 13th, to confer with the Consul and to examine the protocols of a meeting held in Washington nearly two years earlier, to settle the Samoan question. After five years of conflict, United States Secretary of State Thomas F. Bayard had called a conference with the British and German ministers to try to settle outstanding differences among the Western nations regarding trade and protection of citizens in the Kingdom of Samoa. So uncertain had been the results that in the summer of 1887 Bayard had "recessed" the meetings, hoping that the British and Germans would come back later in the year with more acceptable solutions to the problem of Samoan independence and the rights of the three powers. The Germans had been taking the initiative ever since, and Admiral Kimberly was not quite certain what had been done and what ought to be done. The Admiral did know that he must make a strong show of force at this particular time. He had not been sent from the Western Hemisphere to back down before the expansionist foreign policy of the Kaiser and his empire-maker, Prince Bismarck. But for performance of his task he needed time to study the situation. Several noble Samoan personages suggested that they wanted to stage a feast for the American Admiral, but he shook them off. The time for feasting would come after the problem with the Germans had been settled, he said.

Coal was in short supply in the American fleet. The ships had come so quickly from the West Coast of the United States to respond to this emergency that they had no time to arrange for extra coal supplies. All the coal in Apia had to be brought in from abroad, and most of the supply was in German hands. The New Zealand firm of William Mac-Arthur and Company might be expected to supply the Americans, as well as the British warship, but the MacArthur coal dump was extremely low at this time because of the past spate of bad weather and uncertainties of shipping, and the price was outrageously high, $18 per ton, almost twice the usual amount.

The bunkers of the Admiral's ships were not empty, by far. The Americans had enough coal to steam back to Hawaii without difficulty. But their mission was to remain in Samoan waters until the vexing political and military questions should be solved. The Admiral could not justify using any more coal than necessary, and in any weather but a severe storm he would stay in harbor and ride out the blow at anchor.

So again on March 14th the Admiral sent his flag lieutenant ashore to talk to Consul Blacklock, the MacArthur manager, Mr. Fletcher, British Consul de Coetlogon, and others in the Anglo-American colony. Again he was reassured that this was typical weather for Samoa at the end of the summer season and that there was nothing to worry about.

Yet by midnight on March 14th the Admiral was worried enough to order his ships to start up fires in one boiler, to be ready to use steam to keep from dragging anchor in the worsening sea. It was overcast and raining. The wind was blowing in puffs, varying in direction from southeast to southwest, and in force from two to four (12–24 miles per hour).

During the midwatch, from midnight to four in the morning, the weather took a definite turn for the worse. The barometer dropped from 29.60 to 29.56, and the wind increased to Force 6, then fell off. But since the wind was blowing from a southerly direction, there seemed to be little cause for concern. The Admiral faced the question of getting up more steam in his three ships and came to the same conclusion as before: the weather was not so bad that they could not ride it out in harbor.

The Admiral then had decided to keep his own counsel and play a lone hand. So when he made the decision to remain in Apia harbor in the face of threatening weather, he did not explain to anyone.

Halfway across the harbor from the *Trenton,* Captain Fritze surveyed his ship and the storm that was brewing with a calm gaze. The German sailors began returning from the quay in their boats, rowing furiously in the mounting swell that was covered with chop and spray. From his vantage point on the bridge of the *Adler,* Captain Fritze watched them come. All went well with the men of the *Adler* and the *Olga;* they reached their ships, climbed the Jacob's ladders without incident, and the boats were hoisted inboard, banging, but not seriously, in the increasing roll.

With the men of the *Eber* it was a different story. *Oberbootsmannsmaat* Krause of the *Eber* had been sitting in a bar in the German city east of the Mulivai bridge when he heard the first shots from the flagship. Quickly he had moved outside and with a glance at the threatening sky had hurried up and down the street, peering into every store and bar, collaring his men and shoving them down to the dockyard at the edge of the West Harbor.

In all, the Bo'sun found some twenty men, quite a crowd for his longboat and not all of them in shape to row or even stand unassisted, but they had to get back together. He hustled the men into the boat and cast off, aware that in the hour that had passed since he heard the guns the sky had become almost as dark as night and the wind had freshened considerably. The ten oars flashed raggedly in the swell and chop; the boat heaved and bucked, and zigzagged its way around Cape Horn and toward the *Eber,* anchored, as luck would have it, as far away from the dockyard as she could be.

It was a long and tortured journey, and *Oberbootsmanns-maat* Krause was not always certain they would make it safely, but by three o'clock they were in sight of the *Eber.* At three o'clock this meant they were only a few yards from their ship, the darkness of night had set in, and the rain was coming down in sheets that cut normal vision by at least half.

They pulled up to starboard, amidships, where the Jacob's ladder bumped snakily against the hull, and then out five feet, the lower rung grazing the wave tops as it tossed, and the ladder shivering in the wind. The Bo'sun saw that he had a new problem; how was he to get his men up that ladder?

Bo'sun Krause could be thankful for small favors; at least the long ride in the cold rain had sobered up all his men so there was not a drunk in the gang.

"*Raus,*" he ordered them up the ladder, and with a stricken look the first seaman grabbed the rope on the fly and began the long unsteady climb.

The second man made it up safely, and the third, and all those who were passengers, with only one falling off the ladder into the sea and having to be fished out with an oar. The port oars were shipped, and the oarsmen sat in their seats fending off as the ship leaned down to roll over them with the sea. All was well as long as *Oberbootsmannsmaat*

Krause had his crew with him, but when it came time for the oarsmen to leave the boat, life became complicated. Krause himself took a rower's place at port and fended off as the men went up, lively as they could, knowing that now there was a hurry.

The oars were shipped, and Krause and his last five men stayed in the boat as she was hooked to the davits and the hoisting began. There was one awful moment: the davit falls were hooked to the hoisting rings, but loose, the oars were shipped and the fenders inboard when a gust caught the longboat and slapped it against the ship's side with a crash that made Krause's eyes blink and shook every timber in the boat. But she held, and in five minutes the men were standing on deck, grinning in the happiness of safety.

All morning long the wind had been blowing from a southerly direction, which meant that it had come down to the ships over Apia mountain. The gusts and puffs and the rain in the wind indicated to the old salts that a gale was blowing on the south side of the island, but until noon the harbor itself had been relatively quiet, with only the swell increasing. In the first three hours of afternoon, however, the wind switched to northeast, which meant it was blowing almost straight into the harbor mouth, and then the dishpan anchorage began to kick up with a fury. By three o'clock the wind had shifted to due north, which meant it was coming straight down the slot, from the mouth of the harbor, trying to force the ships against the sharp reef that nearly encircled them.

Lieutenant Allen had the watch again aboard the *Trenton*, and he noted laconically that "at 3 wind came out fresh from N.E., shifting to North and blowing from moderate breeze to moderate gale in squalls." What he did not say was that the rain was coming down pell-mell, that the waves had grown as high as the top of a house, and that as the sea fell back from shore, the top of the ugly reef was bared to warn the men-of-war.

A typhoon had borne down on the Samoan Islands. Between two and three o'clock in the afternoon the center of the storm passed a little to the north of Apia harbor. The barometer fell to 29.07, and the old Samoa hands later discovered there had not been a storm like that one at least since 1851, and perhaps never.

The gusty winds that came over the mountain from the south at midday were the front quadrants of the typhoon, and the strong gale that began blowing at three o'clock in the afternoon of March 15th represented the rear quadrants.

This storm had originated in the southeast trade winds that blew during the summer months from a high-pressure belt running roughly between Australia and Chile, with an anticyclonic system located eastward of the island and another westward. The southeast trades blew toward the equatorial or low-pressure region, and sometimes when conditions were just right, as they were on March 13th, enormous whirlwinds rotating clockwise swept across the sea, moving away from the equator along a great parabolic orbit toward the anticyclone west of Chile.

As the center of the storm passed Samoa, the glass began to rise rapidly, which was some comfort to the captains on their bridges. The wind was troublesome, and it would take careful use of steam to ease up the strain on the anchors if that northerly wind continued to blow, but in a few hours the storm would have moved away and the harbor would quiet down. It was not so much unlike the other storms of the summer, even though the barometer had fallen lower.

For a few moments at around two o'clock it was almost dead calm in the harbor, under a leaden sky, and then had begun the waves that nearly swamped *Oberbootsmannsmaat* Krause. The calm of 2 P.M. had been the traditional "calm in the eye of the storm."

On the beach during the early afternoon of March 15th the shopkeepers of Apia began moving all their wares inside the stores and closing the shutters tight. Anything loose was either brought in or tied down, carts and carriages were housed, and sun awnings were carefully tied back against the buildings so they would not rip in the rising winds. From the street of Apia in the growing darkness the peak of Apia mountain could no longer be seen. It was as if there had been a total eclipse of the sun.

Along the street and shore the coconut palms began to bend, their fronds fluttering like a thousand birdwings in the howling wind. In the American consulate in the center of Apia, William Blacklock sat down at his desk to write his daily notes.

"The weather looks very bad," he wrote, "the barometer has fallen to 29.10 at 2 P.M. All men of war have steam up. The old timers expect a hurricane during the night. . . ."

Old Samoa settlers, such as the British merchant George Pritchard, looked out at the white-capped harbor and wondered how much longer it would be before the men-of-war hoisted anchor and moved out to sea and safety. There was no question in the minds of Pritchard and the others that this would be the great storm, typhoon, or hurricane, as they might call it. One single fact made the future crystal-clear to the residents: the wind had shifted to the north, and Apia's worst storms always came down from that direction.

Two types of cyclonic storms were common in the Pacific islands. In one type of typhoon the "bull's-eye" or calm space is relatively large, and the strongest winds are found in an annular space around it, but at a considerable distance. The second type of storm has a smaller "bull's-eye" and much fiercer winds whirling about it; this second storm is infinitely more dangerous at its center than the first.

Fortunately for the men-of-war in Apia harbor, the March 15th storm was of the first or gentler variety, although it can be assumed that in the middle of that day the officers and men of the ships were not concerned about such a difference.

Admiral Kimberly looked out at the sky and sea in midafternoon, noted the rising barometer with some satisfaction, and prepared to wait out the wind. As far as he could see, there was no danger to his ship. It would save coal to stay at anchor, and from the looks of the political situation, he might need all the coal he could forage, so he must save every sooty chunk in his bunkers. Besides, he was half-committed now to stay in port, whether he liked it or not. He could scarcely hoist anchors in these seas, in this wind, without the danger of losing a bower. Such loss would mean an inquiry and a great deal of trouble. It was not a major consideration in anything that affected the safety of the ship, but it was a consideration.

Under normal conditions, in Apia harbor at high water one saw only the water up to the edge of the shore road that ran around from Matautu Point on the east to Mulinuu on the west, and behind the road the houses, consulates, shops, and churches of the foreign community. At low tide one could see the flat red surface of the coral reef, standing up like a plain, with lumps of coral sticking up above shallow pools of limpid water.

When the wind blew from the north, even lightly, the surf came booming up on the coral reef from Matautu to Malinuu, with a noise so loud that people in the beachside houses could not carry on normal conversation. On March 15th, beginning in midafternoon, the surf pounded the coral with a deafening boom that grew more pronounced hour by hour. The water smashed against breakwaters and docks, sending clouds of spray twenty feet in the air; the wind caught the spray and dashed it against the roofs and into the verandas of the houses. The palms swayed more rapidly, their fronds rustled more noisily, and here and there coconuts began to drop.

CHAPTER SIX

The Ships

As THE WIND kicked up spindrift and the seas rose even higher, the worriers and the superstitious among the sailors of the American fleet began to remember unhappy little details of the past. The *Trenton*, according to official talk, was the best of the wooden ships remaining in the United States Navy. The *Trenton* was a jinx ship, said the superstitious, jinxed from the moment her keel was laid.

She had been built at the New York Navy Yard under the supervision of Naval Constructor S. H. Pook, from designs drawn by Chief Constructor Isaiah Hanscom. All during her building there had been snags, and when they went to launch her on December 30, 1875, she would not slide down the ways. In two hours they could move her only eight feet. For two weeks it had been raining steadily in New York, and the timbers and rollers were all swollen. That was the official reason for the failure. Sailors had another. This wood did not wish to be a ship and refused to move. She would never be a good ship.

Two days later, on New Year's Day, the rain had stopped and *Trenton* was launched successfully. Then she was placed

in dry dock to be fastened, and after that, when she was re-
floated she leaked. Just so, said the superstitious; she was
doing everything possible to keep from becoming a ship.

The Navy put *Trenton* back in dry dock and repaired her
leaks, after which she was taken to the Ninth Street pier
on the East River to receive her machinery. As they were
lowering the high-pressure cylinder into place, the slings
gave way and the cylinder fell fifty feet into the bottom of
the ship, damaging hull and cylinder seriously. Again the
superstitious ones wagged their heads and vowed never to
sail on the *Trenton*.

Then there was the matter of the hawsepipes, which any
able-bodied seaman knew ought to have vented onto the
gun deck instead of below on the berth deck. Even though
on her maiden voyage she had sailed through the Strait of
Magellan like a lamb, with never a split spar or torn sail,
the superstitious were not convinced that the *Trenton* would
be anything but trouble.

The *Vandalia* was the kind of ship men of the modern
Navy detested. She had been an 800-ton sloop of war, and
she had been rebuilt at Boston in 1873 as a 2,100-ton steam
sloop. The "rebuilding" was a guise; in the wave of revulsion
at the end of the Civil War, Navy Secretary Robeson had
been able to keep a force afloat only by "repairs" to ships,
for Congress would not commission new hulls. How much
better it would have been to start from scratch than to create
a monster—an underpowered monster, at that—but the Navy
Department was doing the best it could, and hating the ship
did not help; she was in commission, and someone had to
work her. But for the old salts, real terror came in February
on the voyage out to Samoa. The ship boasted a large black
cat, which had the run of the forecastle and even lorded it
over the main deck. One night in heavy weather the cat was
lost overboard. The next day the sailing-ship men of the

Vandalia began spitting nervously over the side and making little signs to ward off bad luck. The death of the ship's cat, they said, could mean nothing but evil to the *Vandalia*. Mainmastman Ambrose darkly predicted a major disaster, and Chief Quartermaster Brown took it upon himself to warn the midshipmen, who were too innocent to know of the danger.

The *Nipsic* was another post-Civil War re-rig, but her problem was more than superstition. She was not a very happy ship. Commander Mullan was far from a favorite of the naval high command. He had been shunted aside onto the inactive list for four years when the Navy was cut down after the war, although he was a Regular Navy officer. Such treatment meant that somewhere along the line he had been given a bad fitness report and it had blighted his career. He was a staunch, if colorless, officer, but his demeanor was not that kind that made men willing to risk their lives for him.

If one could disregard nationalities, as the weather was most certainly doing, then it had to be said that the most unfortunate of all the ships was the little German *Eber*, which had no business being anchored in Apia harbor in the stormy season of late summer.

Eber had covered the withdrawal of the 140 men of the *Olga* on December 18th, and her landing party, under *Oberbootsmannsmaat* Krause, had rescued the badly mauled Germans from the house on the estate at Fangali. Thereafter the *Eber* had been busy island-hopping for a number of weeks, and carrying mail and dispatches to various German outposts, before settling down in Apia harbor in January.

She had ridden out the storm of February 10th, when the topsail schooner *Matuatu* had been cast up on the reef along with two inter-island sailers, a 44-ton schooner and the cutter *Tituan*. She had seemed to be faring well enough in the storm of February 14th, when the *Constitution* and a Samoan

trading schooner were sunk, but midway in that storm her
anchors had slewed around, and the chain of one had been
fouled in her propeller. She was sliding steadily into the
reef, and the engines could not be used to stop her. With
great presence of mind, *Kapitänlieutenant* Wallis had let her
slide until she was almost on the reef, and the fouling chains
had slipped by the propeller. Then he had put on a burst
of steam and engaged the screws. He had almost come off
scot-free, but not quite. The propeller struck the reef a
glancing blow, which bent one blade and made her thereafter
only half efficient. *Eber* had ridden out the storm of March
7th without trouble, but that storm had been much more
severe on Tutuila, where a number of island schooners were
sunk. Here she was now on the afternoon of March 15th,
with 10-knot engines and a 5-knot screw. No one could call
that lucky.

Olga had been bedeviled, too, with bad luck or what might
be called the fortunes of war. The fifty bluejackets in the
landing party's boats and ninety more in the big pram that
had carried out the landing of December 18th were all her
men—which meant the casualties were hers, too. Three young
officers had gone off on this expedition under *Kapitänlieutenant* Jaeckel. The others were Lieutenants Spengler, Sieger,
and Burchard. As noted, Sieger was first wounded and then
killed by a stray shot as he lay a casualty in the plantation
manor. Spengler was badly wounded and died a few days
after the fight. Burchard was wounded and put out of action.
Thirteen of the *Olga*'s seamen were killed, and another forty
were hurt. The day following the fight, unlucky *Olga* transferred her wounded to the *Eber,* and she transported them
to Auckland hospital and requested immediate support of
reinforcements for the German force.

So only *Adler* and *Calliope* could be said to be happy ships
without complaint against their world. They seemed to be

in condition to do successful battle, with man or with nature.

Surprisingly enough, *Trenton*, the largest ship in the harbor, was the first to feel the force of the storm. Lieutenant Richard Scott had the watch again at four o'clock in the afternoon when the breeze blew up to a moderate gale in squalls, varying from the north-northeast to northeast. The barometer continued to rise, and by sunset (although they could not see the sun) it had risen to 29.27. At 7:57 the *Trenton*'s port bower chain parted in a fresh squall. Immediately the Admiral and the Captain were informed, while Lieutenant Scott rang the engine-room signal to start the ship ahead.

Had all things been equal, Admiral Kimberly must have acknowledged himself temporarily defeated by nature and raised steam to escape the harbor for the sea. It was too late. He could see nothing through the rain and darkness, although the other ships had their anchor lights lit, as did *Trenton*. Where a few hours ago one might have said the warships were together in a snug fit in the harbor, as the wind and sea rose, their juxtaposition became frightening. No one dared move for fear of ramming friend or foe.

It promised to be a nasty night.

CHAPTER SEVEN

The Longest Night

Two minutes after the *Trenton*'s port anchor broke loose, the ship was moving slowly forward, and at eight o'clock she let go her port sheet anchor, abaft the bitts, veering to 60 fathoms. Immediately Captain Farquhar ordered the chains of the starboard bower veered to 60 fathoms also, so that she began riding to the starboard bower and the port sheet, head into the wind. It was not an easy maneuver at 8 p.m. The seas were running very high, throwing spray on the main deck, and the *Trenton* rolled and pitched. Sixty fathoms was about a quarter more chain than she had out before the loss of the port bower. She had been anchored with 52 fathoms on the port bower and 45 fathoms on the starboard with the sheet anchor under the foot, but her new anchorage seemed slightly better than the one she had just left, if anything, even though a sheet anchor was no match for a bower.

During this watch the ghost of the dead ship's cat seemed to settle on the *Vandalia*. She was moored with her anchors northeast by east and southwest by west, with the starboard anchor well over toward the eastern reef. Like *Trenton,* she

66

was really not in the harbor, but in the mouth of it, and thus was taking heavier seas than the more fortunate ships inshore. The wind was so strong, and its currents shifted so trickily, that shortly after eight o'clock the chain on the starboard bower was cracked like a whip in the gale, and when the ship was taut against the anchor once again, there was an elbow in the hawse, which meant the links were crosswise instead of straight on, a condition in which the strength of the chain was lessened greatly. In normal weather the difficulty was simple enough to remedy, but not in a storm, with perhaps worse weather yet to come. There was really nothing at all to be done about it.

All the preparations had been made for the evil night ahead: *Vandalia's* top-hamper was down, which meant the topmasts and yards would neither offer undue resistance to the wind nor crack off to endanger the men below. Her battery was secured for sea, which meant the guns would not roll on the decks and crash through bulkheads or the hull itself. Fires were lighted under four of the six boilers for steam. One other boiler was already in use, distilling water for the ship. From the point of view of Chief Engineer Greene in the engine room, everything on *Vandalia* was shipshape, and he settled down to take the watch himself, while his assistant, Engineer Harrie Webster, turned in at ten o'clock for a few hours of sleep before he relieved the Chief. Engineer Webster took the precaution of dogging down the porthole in his cabin, but only because experience in Apia had taught him that it was always unsafe to keep the betweendeck air ports open. In a moment he was sound asleep.

Abovedecks the men of the *Vandalia* did not feel nearly as secure as the black gang, for while the ship was riding well at her anchors, the officers could sense a gradual worsening of the weather, and they were far too close to *Calliope* for comfort. Midshipman Henry A. Wiley had the evening watch

on the forecastle, and he stood on deck watching the sea
clutching ever higher at the hull of his ship, drenched in the
rain in spite of his oilskins, the water running down his neck
and down his nose.

Calliope was anchored inside *Vandalia* and slightly astern,
her port to the American ship's starboard. Midshipman
Wiley glanced at her anxiously from time to time, but her
anchors were holding as well as Captain Kane had expected
them to do, and there seemed to be no danger from that
score. *Vandalia*'s chains were clanking ominously, but they
could scarcely be heard above the growing sound of the wind.

As for *Calliope,* she was not without her own difficulties.
Earlier in the day she had steamed around her anchors to
take the turns out of their cables, but well before midnight it
seemed that she might just as well have forgone the effort.
The heavy sea running through the funnel entrance of the
harbor was causing every ship to plunge heavily and sheer
with wild abandon, and was coiling up kink after kink in
the chain.

As the hours went by and the surf thundered down on the
reefs, that same force came slapping against *Calliope*'s rudder.
The ship's wheel had been manned early in the evening
watch to keep her head to wind and sea, but as she had no
steam steering gear, the yawing and the smashing blows
against her rudder caused the wheel to become completely
unmanageable.

Captain Kane sent men between decks to connect the spare
tiller and reeve wheel-ropes to it, and the spare wheel and
the relieving tackles were then manned. In that way *Calliope*
could be managed and the strain relieved.

U.S.S. *Nipsic* had secured one of the most protected and
favored anchorages by virtue of the old sea rule that first
gets best. She was anchored with the sandy beach to her
starboard, close off Matautu Point, with *Olga* on her port

beam. Early in the day *Eber* had been on *Nipsic's* port quarter, but she had slipped in the hours since afternoon, until now she was astern of *Nipsic* and far closer than either Commander Mullan or *Kapitänlieutenant* Wallis liked. *Nipsic* was riding to three anchors, port and starboard bowers and a starboard sheet anchor. Well before midnight, all three anchors were veered to their full scopes; Captain Mullan had done all he could to avoid collision with either of his German neighbors.

Neither he nor any of the other captains could see more than a few feet in the Stygian blackness, nor could anyone on shore see any of the vessels in the harbor that night.

By eleven o'clock the wind was very strong. Captain Kane of the *Calliope* said it was blowing a full gale, although *Nipsic's* log showed the wind variable between Force 7 and Force 9.

When the barometer had begun to rise in the afternoon, all the captains had believed the gale was about to break and that the wind would haul around to the west. Instead, it remained in the northeast quadrant.

As the midwatch began in the early minutes of March 16th, the barometer continued to rise, and the captains continued to hope that at any moment the storm would move away and give them respite, before serious damage came to the ships.

Ensign J. J. Blandin had the watch on board the flagship, and he reported the worsening weather. The *Trenton* began swinging between north-northeast and northeast by east as the wind shifted, for she was on long cable. The *Trenton* was rolling heavily and pitching against her anchors so that at 12:50 it was necessary to signal the engine room for power and to move slow ahead under steam to keep the strain off the starboard bower, which was the *Trenton's* major weapon in this battle against the sea.

Rough as the sea had become, it was not so much a matter of concern to Admiral Kimberly as the barometer, which was behaving in a thoroughly disagreeable and totally confusing manner. Having risen during the evening, and leveled off at 29.40 during the middle watch, it now fell, then rose again. Admiral Kimberly could not account for it. Captain Farquhar could not explain the phenomenon, either, nor could Lieutenant R. M. Brown, the navigator of the *Trenton*.

The unsavory behavior of the glass indicated three possibilities to Admiral Kimberly. First, they might be so unfortunate this night as to have two storms to contend with instead of one. A single hurricane or typhoon would have behaved as did this storm up until the middle watch, but then the barometer should have kept rising, and it had stopped, instead. So something was amiss, and two storms, one traveling on the tail of the other, would account for the difference.

Or, it might be a single storm that was recurving. Hurricanes and typhoons were known to be extremely eccentric, and on occasion they struck a point, went out to sea, then turned around and came back with fiendish accuracy to strike the same place once again.

Finally, and this latter was the solution Admiral Kimberly considered to be most likely, the storm might have been generated directly over the mountains of Samoa and could be making little progressive movement. If that was the case, they did not know what to expect, for the barometer was no help to them; it did not square with the known habits of tropical storms.

Whatever the problem, Admiral Kimberly and his senior officers now all expected further difficulty, for they had been very close to the eye of the storm, if not actually in it, and the center meant trouble. The Admiral could recall hearing of the great storm of 1844 that had crossed directly over

Havana harbor, causing seventy-two vessels to founder at their anchors, although the port was considered the safest in the Western Hemisphere.

Actually, the storm that was threatening them was a single storm. Its center, having passed Apia between two and three o'clock in the afternoon, was far out at sea, heading westward. On its track it was encountering another hurricane of equal or greater severity, in the same latitude as Samoa, roughly 14° S., but 25 degrees of longitude to the west of the islands. The presence of this other storm caused the Samoa typhoon to recurve and move back along its track toward Apia harbor. The rise and fall and rise again of the barometer in the middle of the night represented the turning of the storm, even as the senior officers of the ships began to hope for the best.

Although the Admiral and the Captain hoped to see bettering weather with the coming of the dawn, Ensign Blandin was ordered to free the ship's prisoners from the brig—just in case something untoward might occur in the next few hours. The Ensign went below, released the guard and opened the barred door to the brig, then told the four men inside to look sharp and return to duty.

The *Vandalia*'s situation around midnight was more precarious than that of the flagship. Captain Schoonmaker was not pleased with the functioning of his engines, but for that matter, they had never been strong enough for the ship, and there was little he could do about that problem in the middle of a storm. Without anyone's noticing it, *Vandalia* began to slip a little, moving toward *Calliope*. Shortly after midnight, this dragging caused *Vandalia* to move directly in the hawse of the *Calliope,* making it dangerous to veer her anchors any farther, which meant she would have to rely more on steam than ever. Seven of the eight boilers were lighted, and they furnished all the steam the ship could use, for the engines were used intermittently, at speeds varying from 18 to 42 revolutions.

At one o'clock on the morning on March 16th, Chief Engineer Greene sent an oiler to rout out Engineer Webster and tell him it was time for him to come on watch. In a moment Webster was on his feet and dressing. He passed through the wardroom on his way to the engine room and saw the Chief Engineer in deadly serious conversation with Paymaster Arms. The Paymaster was in his nightgown—so odd a costume for the wardroom that Engineer Webster had an uncomfortable feeling that all was not as it ought to be.

In the stuffy warmth of the engine room Engineer Webster methodically checked his engines and boilers and then climbed up to the top platform, where he had a view of everything going on in the department. The engines were running slowly but steadily, but one could not say such gentle words about the ship. She was pitching and rolling and pulling up short against her anchors with such a snap that it was impossible to maintain firm footing in the engine room without a handhold.

At this time the *Vandalia* began taking heavy waves, and her conduct was such that Lieutenant James Carlin, the ship's executive officer, took the deck himself. A few moments later came the call "All hands on deck!" and the crew mustered to do what might be done to fight the storm.

Midshipman Henry Wiley ran messages from Carlin's position on the poop deck and the forward part of the ship, for that was the only way the executive officer's commands could be made known. Carlin was shouting into the teeth of a gale, and his words were whisked behind him as they came out of his mouth.

Crewmen strung lifelines along the waist of the *Vandalia*, and young Wiley stumbled and ran, sometimes even crawling, with the seas washing over him and threatening every moment. To stay on the open deck was suicidal, so officers and crew huddled under the poop or forecastle or shivered in the waist. The moment he stepped on deck, every man was soaked to the skin, but there was nothing to be done about that. Every man had his job, and there was not time to worry about anything but salvation.

The smaller *Nipsic* had begun to suffer earlier from the strong winds and high seas, even though she was considered to have the most favorable anchorage in the harbor. Beginning at midnight the seas were breaking over her in spray, and she was rolling and yawing considerably. To keep out of the way of *Olga* and *Eber,* the *Nipsic* steamed full ahead constantly.

By midnight *Nipsic*'s anchors had begun to slip, and Captain Mullan ordered the starboard chains heaved in. At 12:30 the work began. The starboard anchor was brought in, and then the sheet anchor was hove in to four fathoms on the starboard chain. By this time the smaller ships in the harbor were bobbing like corks and yawing dangerously toward the reefs. Dark as it was, the schooner *Lily* came in sight on the port bow—and then vanished. *Olga* could be seen dimly on the port quarter, and *Eber,* unfortunately, could be seen only too well astern, for at times she seemed to be about to come aboard. About 2:30 in the morning Captain Mullan saw a signal of distress from one of the merchant barques moored westward of her. He did not know it, but what he was witnessing at the time was the collision of the German barque *Peter Godeffroy* and *Santiago,* the Norwegian sailing ship moored near her. The squalls and the constant blowing of spindrift made it impossible to see what was happening.

As for the other merchant vessels, trading schooners, and island craft, most of the captains and crews had simply gone aboard in midafternoon and set extra anchors, then had returned to shore to leave the fates of their vessels in the hands of the sea. Here again was indication of the surprising nature of this particular storm, coming as late in the season as it did, and under such strange circumstances.

Ashore on this night of storm the lights burned brightly in the consulates. Dr. Knappe, who suffered from New Guinea fever, still stayed up late, worrying over his dispatches and the fate of the German ships in the harbor. His position was serious, but not desperate if the German reinforcements arrived in time to put down Mataafa and install Tamasese. Dr. Knappe had gone far in making German policy, pushed by commercial interests with his Emperor's obvious approval. The disapproval of Chancellor Bismarck meant the end of Knappe's career unless he was able to present his government with a *fait accompli*.

The consulate was guarded by armed sailors at the doors, and other armed sailors patrolled the streets of Matafele, the German quarter, to assure the safety of the German colonists from attack by Mataafa. Fifty sailors from the three German ships were detailed ashore to this task.

The English consulate was unguarded. Colonel de Coetlogon, the consul, had sent the armed guard back to the *Calliope* five days earlier. With the Americans in the harbor, affairs had taken a different turn, and he could afford to be rid of the sailors. They were something of a nuisance, under the circumstances, because the de Coetlogons had turned their consulate into a hospital. The German Naval Hospital stood on the shore between the stone Evangelical Church and Mr. Moors's Tivoli Hotel, but the Naval Hospital did not treat Mataafa's Samoans. When the fighting had broken out between Mataafa and Tamasese, and then the Germans had joined in, the sight of festering wounds and gangrene had sickened the de Coetlogons. Backed by the English and American communities, they had made their consulate into a hospital where all could be treated, and on this night several dozen of Mataafa's wounded followers were lying on mats in the downstairs rooms. Usually the sick and wounded were housed on the veranda or under tents on the lawn. But with a wind blowing inshore so strongly that already the coconut trees on the beach had been stripped of their fronds, no tent could stand, and the patients had been evacuated inside during the afternoon.

Mrs. de Coetlogon and her assistant, Miss Taylor, were on their evening rounds, dosing a high chief with brandy when he complained of pains (nonexistent, they were sure) that wracked his belly. The Samoan warrior Siteone, whose shoulder blade had been smashed in the first engagement, lay on a mat in one corner, demanding attention; he was the spoiled patient of the hospital, for he had been there longer than any of the others.

At the American consulate, a few feet to the east of the English consulate-hospital, William Blacklock added to his dispatches for Secretary of State Blaine the fact that the wind had increased that night to gale force, and then settled down to sleep as best he could and wait for the coming of the dawn, hopeful that the American ships would ride out the storm safely. Lieutenant Fillette, the Marine Corps officer in charge of the 20-man Marine guard, posted his guards, and he, too, waited.

In his house in the Samoan city outside Apia, High Chief Seumanu Tafa lay in the darkness, listening to the wind. His pretty niece, the willowy, raven-haired maiden Fanua, was frightened of this storm that threatened their island. On the southwest tip of the island, however, the people of the village of Faleata went to sleep without care, for they had experienced no more than a slightly heightened breeze during the evening.

Nine o'clock on Friday evening was the hour for chorus singing at the Evangelical Church near the German Naval

Hospital, and several dozen Christian Samoans and a sprinkling of foreign missionaries appeared on schedule and carried out their practice, although the pump organ and the voices were sometimes drowned out by the noises of the storm, wind howling and waves crashing on the coral reef.

Apia's reef possessed acoustical qualities quite above and beyond those of the other Pacific islands in the area. The Mulivai and the Vaisingano (*vai* means river in Samoan) created currents of their own in the harbor. Over a thousand years these currents had acted with the tides and storms to undermine the reef and give it an overhanging edge. Once created, this overhang made currents and undertows of its own, so that Apia harbor was difficult for swimming, even on a calm day when the white sand sparkled against the green of the mountains, the brown of the coconut palms, and the clear blue of the sky. On a night like this Friday night, with the wind howling across the shore road so forcefully that a man could not stand unaided against it, the currents were stronger and more unpredictable than ever.

To add to the difficulties of the ships in the harbor, at about midnight came a new threat from the land, one the men of the sea could not have anticipated and could not control even if they had recognized it.

For twenty-four hours it had been raining almost steadily. At first, in the hours before Friday's dawn, it had rained fitfully on the beach and in the harbor, with the storm coming over the mountains from the south. Those mountains received more rain than the northern shore of the island. Then the storm had switched and moved around to the northeast, with heavier rain coming ashore and striking the north slope of the mountains as well as the coastline.

Long before midnight, the ground everywhere had been soaked to saturation and the rain was making its way back to the sea in the normal runoff channels. The Mulivai, usually a gentle brook, was now an impressive river. The Vaisingano, a river, had become a raging torrent. In years past, the rivers had brought silt down from the mountain with their gentle flow and had carpeted the reef at the bottom of the harbor with a coat of soil in which ocean plants grew and where a ship's anchor could find purchase. By Friday midnight the rushing current of the Vaisingano had scoured a broad channel through this sea bottom, revealing the harsh and impenetrable coral reef, on which ships' anchors could only slide. Naturally the scouring began at the innermost point of the harbor, and thus what had been considered the safest part of the haven became the most dangerous. The discharge of the powerful spume of Vaisingano aimed toward Cape Horn, clearing out the bottom next to the infamous Shore Reef on which already lay one old wreck in warning.

On the midwatch even *Calliope* with her oversized anchors was beginning to feel the effects of the gale from the north-northeast. At two o'clock Captain Kane had the feeling that the ship was beginning to drag anchor, and he responded by beginning to steam ahead in the squalls. He could not be sure what was happening, because he could not see the reefs or any landmarks; for safety's sake, he ordered steam in the fourth boiler. He did not want to overdo his precautions, so he refrained from letting the sheet anchor go, for he planned to veer the port chain as soon as daylight came, then run out and let the sheet go a good distance from the Shore Reef, which was on the ship's port quarter.

By three o'clock on Saturday morning, March 16th, the wind was blowing what the English called "a furious gale," the barometer continued to fluctuate as the storm turned on its path to recurve and headed back toward Apia, the swell had grown to huge proportions, and the gale was still making, still had not reached its peak. The moon was up, but the heavy clouds completely obscured it, and in the driving rain the men of *Calliope* could see barely twenty feet into the murk.

Long before three o'clock, the *Eber* was in serious difficulty. She had drifted in the beginning of the evening into a position that put her directly in the path of the torrential underwater current from the Vaisingano that was scouring the bottom of the harbor.

"*Alle Mann an Deck!*" Captain Wallis ordered, as he saw the ship slipping toward the reef. *Eber* was, in fact, as far away from the deadly Shore Reef as any ship in harbor save the *Nipsic,* yet from the beginning Captain Wallis had a sinking feeling about the events of the night, and he was quicker than any of the others to respond. Smallest ship though she was, the *Eber*'s men showed no panic as they swung to the not very hopeful task of saving the ship. After all, she was not as large as the *Peter Godeffroy,* which had taken such a beating before colliding with the Norwegian, and although *Eber* had engines, Captain Wallis could not rely on them. After the storm of February 14th, when he had actually been saved in a hairbreadth escape when literally hanging on the rim of the reef, *Olga* had taken *Eber* in tow and pulled her safely out of the harbor to ride out the storm. Tonight *Olga* was thoroughly occupied with her own affairs, and *Eber* would have to live or die through the efforts of her own crew alone.

Tiny *Eber* was so defenseless; before midnight the waves were slapping over her decks, drenching every man, and wetting the ship from stem to stern, inside and out. *Kapitän-lieutenant* Wallis had the bridge, and his First Officer, *Lieutenant zur See* Eckardt, had the deck. The navigator was *Lieutenant zur See* von Ernsthausen, and the adjutant was *Unterlieutenant zur See* Gaedeke. *Eber* carried her own doctor, *Assistenzarzt* Dr. Wachenhauer, her paymaster,

Marine-Unterzahlmeister Kunze, and her engineering officer, *Obermaschinist* Teuber.

Every officer was at his post. From the beginning of the evening *Assistenzarzt* Wachenhauer was fully occupied, caring for the sick of the *Eber* in the tiny sickbay, and treating the cuts and bruises of the men who were being slammed around the deck like so many ninepins in a giant game of bowls.

Around midnight the *Eber* began pulling heavily on her anchor chain. Captain Wallis had much earlier ordered steam, but he was hesitant to use his mangled propeller, so he applied the engines seldom and only in short snatches, relying more on the strength of his chains than on his power.

Oberbootsmannsmaat Krause and two sailors stood at the helm, the three of them straining at the wheel to keep *Eber*'s rudder pointing her into the wind, as the Captain ordered the engines engaged. Every few minutes a particularly wrenching wave would send the wheel a few points to port or starboard, in spite of the strength of the three sailors; there was no pattern to it—the storm seemed to change its thrust constantly.

Midway in the middle watch, Captain Wallis was standing on the *Kommandobrücke,* or command bridge, his face gray and stern, handling the engine telegraph carefully, and gazing out into the faceless sea as though he could see something there when no one else could make out a single object.

Suddenly there came a huge, sharp jolt that shook the ship from stern to stem. Men went tumbling across the deck, grasping desperately at the lifelines, as the heavy pooping sea rushed aboard the ship. A dozen men were completely covered by the foamy green-black water, and they came up coughing and spitting and swearing at the sea. But they did come up, and not a man was lost overboard, miracle though it seemed; nonetheless, that furious wave had done the storm's dirty work; the starboard anchor chain had parted in the shock of the pooping wave, which had smashed against the stern.

Captain Wallis's face turned dead white. The ship was driving forward, onto the eastern reef, the port anchor dragging. For a moment there was silence, as he gripped the rail with one hand, as if to stave off that slipping. Then he pulled himself together.

"Maschine auszerste Kraft zuruck," he signaled—full speed back.

The Captain released the telegraph and stood with both hands on the rail, his face like stone, waiting.

The engines engaged and roared, but nothing happened. The screw had failed!

In a moment First Officer Eckardt was on the bridge, reporting. The broken starboard anchor chain had wrapped itself around the screw, he said. The seamen forward had seen it slacken as the cable broke, then tighten, and now the chain was fast, pulled snug along the starboard buttock. There could be no doubt about it.

The port anchor was not holding, or it was holding just enough to slew the *Eber* around and put her in the deadly position of broadside to the gale.

Captain Wallis's lips tightened. There was only one chance for salvation, and that a very slim one. The engine ratios for reversing gave the *Eber* perhaps a third of the power that she could generate at full forward speed.

"Auszerste Kraft voraus!" the Captain shouted and signaled to the engine room. Full speed ahead!

For a moment the *Eber* seemed almost silent, though the gale howled all about her. She began to tremble as her engines gave power but were resisted by the screw. She shuddered, and then there came a loud *crack* as metal snapped against metal, and the screw began churning, the ship responding to her helm. Turned as she was by the veering of the port anchor, *Eber* gave a wild spring landward, pushed by the following sea, and seemed to be headed straight for the Shore Reef's sharp fangs. But Captain Wallis ordered full right rudder, *Oberbootsmannsmaat* Krause and his two seamen turned a suddenly responsive wheel with all their might; slowly the *Eber* began to put her head into the wind and come about to face the eastern reef again and move back across the narrow channel away from the lee shore.

First Officer Eckardt reported the starboard chain free and aboard, and being rove to the reserve anchor.

Every man on the bridge gave a little sigh of relief at the end of the crisis, and for a moment Captain Wallis appeared almost benign. Then he was ordering the bridge watch to look sharp and prepare to drop anchor and veer the starboard anchor to suit. The calmness of the orders gave the men of the *Eber* new faith, and they began to believe the little cockleshell of a ship might yet be saved.

CHAPTER EIGHT

Death Knell

AT THREE O'CLOCK on the morning of March 16th, every ship afloat in Apia harbor was dragging her anchors and rolling, pitching, and yawing so strenuously that had the picture been seen from above, it would have appeared as some wild ballet of walnut shells upon a foaming pool. The wind drove the sea on at Force 10—60 miles an hour—still coming in from the north-northeast, but beginning to slide a little toward north, which increased the pressure of the waves. The 226-foot *Olga* was riding well, perhaps because the scouring of the Vaisingano had not yet affected her anchorage. She slipped a little, but by using the engines Captain von Erhardt was able to maintain his position far better than the *Eber* or any of the smaller vessels. The Captain had seen the death signals of the *Peter Godeffroy,* just before she and *Santiago* struck, and he had noted the occurrence for the log. The *Nipsic* was sliding slowly backward, moving toward the Shore Reef across the harbor, and had come to a point off *Olga*'s starboard bow, but was not so close as to worry Captain von Erhardt more than he had been worried before. *Olga*'s engines were responding, she had not lost any anchors, and there seemed every chance of riding out the storm without serious damage, if she was not fouled by another ship.

Korvettenkapitän Fritze's S.M.S. *Adler* was riding off the starboard beam of *Olga,* also not yet affected by the Vaisingano's runaway currents. During the evening watch and until midnight Captain Fritze had refrained from using his engines, although he had steam up in all boilers, and he had taken the bridge himself hours before.

For an hour the careful, painstaking Fritze had been working with the engine telegraph, apparently playing with it, if appearances could be believed. Far from playing, however, the Captain was fingering the points of command—slow ahead, half speed, full ahead, stop, slow astern, full astern. He was finding these positions with his fingers, memorizing them—as if he did not know them by heart—preparing himself for action if the bridge lights should fail. From the port bow the *Adler* was shipping heavy seas, so heavy that the Captain quite expected his lights to fail at any time. The rain mixed with sea spray blew in his face, and the salt stung his eyes so the tears ran down his weathered cheeks.

At 3:45 the Captain's fears were realized: *Adler's* lights failed, and the bridge was plunged into darkness. Without a tremor Captain Fritze spoke reassuringly to his helmsman and remained at his position by the telegraph.

By four o'clock as the watch changed the wind had risen to Force 11 on the Beaufort scale, or more than 66 miles an hour, and had slid around a little more to the north. The barometer had been acting strangely for eight hours, but it began to fall steadily. At one o'clock on Saturday morning the glass had registered 29.32; three hours later, it read 29.25 and was still falling.

As the wind shifted north, the seas grew more severe; the Pacific was certainly misnamed this night; it had a clear sweep of a thousand miles down from the north, and the black waves plunged at the shore, at one moment burying the reef under fathoms of water that sped into the land, throwing the death-dealing salt spray a hundred yards inland from the beach, washing away parts of the road, undermining trees, and blighting the grass and bushes.

The *Trenton* was battened down tightly, riding to three anchors on a long scope of chain, two men at the wheel and all hands on deck. The Admiral was on his bridge, as wet as the most miserable apprentice seaman on the forecastle; the *Trenton* seemed to be holding steady in the heavy seas, but when a wave struck the ship, so great was the new power of the storm that sheets of water were thrown up from the bows, carried by the wind *over* the lower mastheads and smashed down on the deck. The sea was coming inboard so fast that the scuppers could not handle it, and at times a full foot of water ran in the spar deck waterways.

On the bridge, Admiral Kimberly peered about him, unable to make out a ship, unable to see the reef, unable even to determine whether the *Trenton* was dragging anchors. The air was constant with flying spray; the wind added spindrift to the rain and blew it at an angle; the spray struck the Admiral's face with such force that his eyes could not bear the pain of the piercing spatter for long, nor could he look to windward in the gusts. Sometimes he had to turn to catch his breath, the air snatched from his lips by the driving wind.

Shortly after four o'clock, one ferocious sea smashed *Trenton* a shuddering blow, carrying away her head booms and the rudder head, and still the fury of the storm increased. *Trenton* was calving heavily, wallowing deep in the troughs of the waves and rising to the ends of her chains. As she dipped her nose, she began taking tons of water in the bows; it gushed in through the hawseholes and ran splashing into the berth deck. Soon, the *Trenton* was making so much water belowdecks that the First Officer, Lieutenant Commander Henry W. Lyon, reported the unpleasant fact to Captain Farquhar. The sea was attacking *Trenton* in her weak spot.

Outside, behind the American flagship, the *Vandalia* was riding better than Captain Schoonmaker expected. At two o'clock Lieutenant Carlin asked for permission to place the *Vandalia*'s single remaining sheet anchor because he and the Captain could sense that they were drifting, although they could see nothing to indicate the slippage in fact. Carlin had been holding off, waiting for the wind to shift to north or west, but by two o'clock it seemed foolhardy to hold off longer. Permission was granted, the ship steamed ahead to relieve pressure on her starboard anchor, and Lieutenant Carlin placed the sheet as close to the weather reef on the east as he could estimate in the darkness and the surging sea. For the next three hours *Vandalia* also *seemed to be* holding steady, although no one could tell for sure. At four o'clock, when the wind increased, she began shipping waves with such force and regularity that although she was tightly battened down, water began to find its way below. In fact, *Vandalia* was not holding steady at all, but was dragging down on *Calliope,* coming closer every hour, although neither captain could know it in the darkness.

This morning watch of March 16th marked the crucial change in the nature of the storm at Apia. The recurve of the storm center was complete, and it was sweeping back on Samoa. It had changed in nature, too, fitful creation of the elements that it was; the eye or center had tightened, and the winds around that center were stronger than before. As the storm came back for another slash at Apia harbor, it was deadly.

At four o'clock *Calliope* was dragging, too, but only

slightly, and since those heavy anchors still found mud and weeds this far out in the channel, Captain Kane remained confident that he could ride out the storm even in this harbor, which he called "as bad a one as you care to enter." Another point in her favor: because of her modern construction, *Calliope* was taking far less water than any of the other vessels.

At 4:30 Saturday morning, Ensign H. P. Jones, Jr., had the watch aboard the *Nipsic,* and he then began referring to the storm as a hurricane, which meant the wind had reached Force 12—72 miles an hour and higher. *Nipsic* had dragged badly; in the beginning light of dawn Captain Mullan could see *Olga* on her port beam and *Eber* dead astern. To recover stability, Captain Mullan ordered the sheet and starboard bower anchors let go and veered the ship to 37 fathoms. He could veer no more without danger of fouling *Olga* or *Eber,* for the wind and sea were trying to drive him back on *Eber,* and the yawing of the ship took him dangerously close to *Olga* when *Nipsic* strained to port.

Even in 37 fathoms of water, the starboard anchors failed to hold, because *Nipsic* had come directly over the scouring current of the Vaisingano, and there was nothing below her but slippery coral reef.

Nipsic's new maneuver gave the sea more chain on which to snap her, and as she yawed Captain Mullan saw himself coming close to *Olga.*

"Hard to starboard," he ordered the helmsman, and the ship responded to the turning, moving away toward Matautu Point. But here, having changed position, the turning ship sliced directly into the little schooner *Lily* and cut her down.

Three men were aboard the schooner, trying desperately to keep her afloat and out of the way of the warships. One was a trader named Ormsby. Another was the owner, Captain

Douglas. The third man was the Hawaiian mate of the *Lily*, who was also able seaman and galley cook. Ormsby and the Hawaiian were swept overboard by the impact of *Nipsic's* bow-on crash, and both were drowned. Captain Douglas was also thrown into the water as the *Lily* sank swiftly beneath the overhanging reef. Aided by the outrushing current of the Vaisingano, he was swept, not to shore, but seaward, and was thrown up against the bow of the *Olga*, some two hundred yards away. In that moment of contact, Captain Douglas was able to grasp a loosened line hanging from the *Olga's* stem and hoist himself aboard. Captain Douglas saved himself; he had no help, save from the sea; not a man on the *Olga* saw this bit of human flotsam until he came up over the side, a dripping wraith, and collapsed unconscious on the deck.

Having smashed out blindly to starboard, *Nipsic* now yawed sharply to port, carried by the rushing current away from the land, while *Olga* was struck at the same time by a huge wave coming from the sea outside. *Olga's* bow pointed head-on to *Nipsic's* port beam, and fascinated, in the growing light, the crew of the *Nipsic* saw her coming.

"Full speed astern," ordered Captain von Erhardt on the *Olga*.

In a moment the ship began to respond, struggling backward, her propeller spinning in reverse, deep beneath the surface of this following sea. Almost, Captain von Erhardt managed to avoid the fateful collision; almost, but not quite, and *Olga's* bow pushed inexorably against *Nipsic's* port side with a rending crash. *Olga's* jib boom broke off, and then she was away, responding to the engines, backing steadily from the American ship. *Nipsic's* port side amidships was a shambles. The whaleboat's davits had twisted at a crazy angle, spilling the boat down into the sea, where she bobbed, attached to her mother ship by the wreckage of the davits. The dinghy was smashed and hung over the side, half submerged.

Nipsic Lieutenant John M. Hawley led his men to the wreckage, and they cut away the broken timbers of the dinghy. He ordered them to hoist the whaleboat back aboard, and the men strained mightily at the ropes, but with the davits gone, pulling overhand against the suction of the sea was impossible, and after ten minutes of trying, Captain Mullan ordered them to cut away the whaleboat. Knives slashed, the ropes parted, and with a jerk of her bow the whaleboat whirled away past the stern, bound for the harsh coral arms of the Shore Reef.

Nipsic was caught between the surge of the ocean waves coming in nearly from due north, the frenzied current of the Vaisingano, and Lord knew what other forces caused by wind, rain, and the undertow of the sea as it escaped from beneath the lip of the eastern reef. She yawed far inshore toward Matautu, then came back again, speeding to port, without apparent notice of the efforts of her engines to relieve her slipping port anchor. Once again she came broadside on, down on *Olga,* and once again *Olga* reversed her engines to full astern to avoid the helpless gunboat. This time *Nipsic* did not escape so lightly. The battered bow of *Olga* smashed against the American ship's port beam again, but on this second crash the waves had lifted the bow of the larger German ship high above the little American, and the blow was a sliding one, the result like that of a croupier raking chips off a roulette table. *Olga*'s bow smashed away the *Nipsic*'s port main anchor chains, cutting through them as if they were cheese, then raked back, breaking off the smokestack, the after ventilator, and the port main yardarm. The heavy prow battered the *Nipsic*'s mainmast, springing it beyond immediate chance of repair—as if there could be any thought of repair to anything this morning. Back, back, the *Olga*'s bow slid, in this terrifying moment, brushing away the steam launch and the second cutter, crumbling the port rail, flicking off the swifters of the main rigging and the mizzen rigging until only the upper shrouds were left flying in the wind, and finally sweeping off the mizzen topmast head before the *Olga*'s propellers bit deep enough to stop the surge and she backed away again.

The *Adler* lay ahead of the *Olga* and by four o'clock had drifted until she was on the *Olga*'s port bow. When the lights on the ship went out, Captain Fritze ordered torches brought up and lighted, and they flickered in the gale, giving precious little illumination, although they were behind the shield in the wheelhouse. *Kapitänlieutenant* von Arend, the First Officer, requested permission to drop the sheet anchor in the hope that they would not drift farther west, for to the west lay nothing but reef, while on the southeast corner of the harbor was the sand where, if worse came to worst, a ship could ground herself and the crew could have a chance at life. After dropping the sheet anchor First Officer Arend took a detachment below to open the between-deck stoppers; the *Adler* was taking so much sea aboard that the negative effect of opening these ports to the sea was more than offset by the runoff of water from above. Captain Fritze played the engine-room telegraph with the skill of a professional musician on his instrument. *Lieutenant zur See* Oelsner stood by a plumb line on the port side of the bridge, with a signalman at his side, and informed the Captain as to the ship's drift, minute by minute. The signalman carried the messages to the Captain on the other side of the bridge—no one aboard the ships could hear a noise five feet away in the wind and pounding of the surf—and the Captain responded by ordering the ship forward and backward as she strained at her chains. In the gathering light they could soon see the *Olga* on the starboard surging back and forth on quite a different course; one of the remarkable aspects of this storm was the change it made in the ebbs and flows of the harbor's water. The first force was the rising tide, which pushed the ships inshore. This tide was enhanced, to say the least, by the 70- and 80-mile-an-hour winds that pushed the sea from the north. Because of the rain and flooding, the tide was met in two places by the rushing currents of the rivers, moving in the opposite direction and creating whirlpools where the opposing forces met. The suction of the reef created its own currents and whirlpools, and the extra-high seas created riptides. So while part of these unleashed forces of nature were driving *Adler* southwest toward the great Shore Reef, *Olga* seemed to be in the grip of a different set of currents and was driving slowly almost due south, toward the extreme east end of the reef, opposite the German Naval Hospital on shore.

From where Captain Fritze was peering in the light of the dawn, *Olga* seemed to be pitching and yawing madly; he could scarcely imagine how his smaller ship must have appeared from the bridge of *Olga*. He could not see beyond, where *Eber* and *Nipsic* were fighting for their lives, and on his port side he could see only *Calliope*, six degrees off his bow; she seemed more at ease than any of the others, although she was pitching mightily.

At 4:30 in the morning, as the light strengthened, Captain Fritze was able to get a better glimpse of his position, and he became alarmed; the reef was far closer astern than he had believed; all seven warships had drifted halfway across the harbor in the darkness. Captain Fritze ordered full speed ahead. If his anchors were dragging, he would drag them with him away from the teeth of the coral. For the first time since the storm broke, Captain Fritze kept the engine-room telegraph set at full speed. Before, he had played the sea as it rose and fell on his stern, releasing the engines as the screw came surging clear of water, engaging again as it sank into the deep; now he gave engines and propeller no mercy. There was no time for nicety; the lives of 128 officers and men depended on those engines, and they must do their job, or all was lost.

Slowly, groaningly, the *Adler* pulled herself away from the reef, dragging her anchors behind her like huge sweeps. But she could not go far, for in sliding and moving she had been forced southward, and now she was coming up on *Olga's* stern, and the bigger ship's hawse blocked her path. The tumbling anchors sank to the bottom again as Captain Fritze moved the telegraph pointer to slow ahead; this speed just kept *Adler's* head into the wind, and gave her no forward motion; the weight of the anchors on their chains now pulled her back close onto the reef, and the anchors began drifting on the scoured coral bottom once again.

In this brief respite, *Obermaschinist* Goetze came on deck and struggled to the bridge to protest the mistreatment of his engines. When the screw was out of water, the vibration was so tremendous that he feared it would shake the bottom out of the ship or break the shaft, he said. The pounding of the sea was bad enough; he was afraid the plant might break down altogether in a few minutes. They must reduce the steam pressure and go slow on the engines.

Captain Fritze stood by his orders. He sympathized with his engineer, said kindly that he was doing his best, and told him to return below and continue to do what he could. There was no way to relieve the pounding of the seas; the Captain must have full power if the ship was to be saved.

At 4:45 one great gusty squall caught the *Adler* in its vise, and Captain Fritze could feel his ship losing ground in the battle with the reef. Back they went, slithering and yawing, and at 4:50 there was a gentle thud, as the stern of the *Adler* touched the edge of the reef.

"Hard to port!" shouted Captain Fritze to the helmsmen, and they spun the big wheel desperately, so desperately that as the ship moved around, engines pounding and screw thrashing, the steering rope broke.

CHAPTER NINE

The Eber

As THE WHEEL spun idly the two helmsmen stared helplessly at Captain Fritze, absolute despair blackening their faces. The Captain did not waver, although there seemed to be nothing he could do to avert disaster; but the momentum gained in those brief seconds as the ship began turning was enough, for the rudder had held for just that instant that meant the difference between salvation and death. *Adler* put her nose into the wind, her stern swung away from the reef, and the starboard anchor held, caught on some outcropping of the sharp coral bottom. The port quarter of the *Adler* was but a few feet from the reef, but those few feet made all the difference. There was time.

In a moment, without an order having been issued *Lieutenant zur See* Caesar was aft, putting the emergency steering into operation with the help of a dozen men. On the bridge the helmsmen dropped their useless holds on the wheel and began reeving the spare wheel-ropes with desperate speed. In five minutes the repairs were finished, and again *Adler* had a chance to save herself from the storm, if her starboard anchor would hold, if the chains would not part, if Captain

Fritze could keep her helm into the wind, and if she would make at least enough headway to steam ahead and relieve the starboard anchor. There was a question now of slipping to port; *Adler* had slewed around in these last unfortunate minutes so that her port beam was quarter-on to the reef. A few hours earlier this situation would have put her in peril, but the wind had been inching steadily toward true north, and so while she was dangerously close to the Shore Reef just before dawn, the wind tended to drive her south, toward reef and the light at the tongue of the harbor, rather than west toward the near point of the reef.

The torches on the bridge sputtered in the rain as the squalls pelted *Adler* and her crew. They also smoked venomously, but not a man could see a wisp; the howling wind rasped at the fire and whisked the smoke away.

At about 4:30 the sky had begun to lighten, and the vague shapes of other ships came into view, tossing in the harbor, standing on their bows, screws churning the air, then sinking back onto their sterns and throwing their cutwaters at the thundering storm above. Now, just before five o'clock in the morning, Captain Fritze could make out his changed relationship to the other ships: *Eber* bucked and swayed off his starboard quarter; *Olga* lay off his port bow—although *lay* was not the word—*Olga* wallowed in the troughs and charged against the peaks, yawing first to port, then to starboard, then to port again, lumbering, like a huge wounded rhinoceros on a chain.

In the gathering light Captain Fritze watched, enchanted, as *Olga* danced on the waves. He did not know it, but Captain von Erhardt was letting out more cable, trying to veer away from *Nipsic* and avoid smashing her once again. Vaguely, Captain Fritze could see *Nipsic* bounding back and forth across the harbor, east of *Olga*'s starboard bow; and off to port, so far that at least this one ship posed no danger to him, he saw *Calliope,* still well away from the point to the reef south of the old wreck that marked the danger.

As Captain Erhardt's men paid out the cable, a gust threw *Olga* toward her port anchor, she yawed, and a wave slapped her starboard bow; the starboard bow anchor dragged, and *Olga* presented her port beam to *Adler*'s bow.

On his bridge, Captain Fritze's lips narrowed and his face whitened as he stared straight ahead. Fritze need not look behind, for there the reef lay waiting. Only by steaming at full speed could he keep *Adler* off the reef. So he stood, engine telegraph locked at full speed ahead, as the *Olga* bore down on him, knowing as she came that they would strike, yet totally unable to stop the impact.

Olga struck with a crashing blow, splintering *Adler*'s bowsprit with a vibration that sent a shiver along her chine. But that was all; it was a clean blow, with no wrench or tearing; *Olga* moved back, straightening her bow into the wind again, steaming ahead to relieve the strain. But as *Olga* moved forward, Captain Fritze could see the great ragged slash in her port quarter, extending down from the main deck halfway to the waterline, opening what he knew must be the berth deck to the fury of the storm.

On the *Olga* Captain von Erhardt had seen the prow of *Adler* coming up on him, with the same sense of helplessness. "Full steam ahead," he ordered the engine room, but it was no use; the storm would have it otherwise, and though the engines reared and the propeller screamed, the sea had pushed *Olga* back inexorably, spitting her on *Adler*'s bowsprit. As *Adler* seemed to back off, and *Olga* steamed hard astarboard, Captain von Erhardt waited impatiently for *Kapitänlieutenant* Jaeckel to report the damage. Jaeckel appeared, saluted, and gave his news: two of *Olga*'s guns had been destroyed, the port cutter had been demolished and the davits battered to the deck, the mizzenmast's lower yard was smashed, the ship was taking water in the lower decks from the hole, but only in the troughs, and the pumps were being manned. Damaged, yes, but Captain von Erhardt could still thank God that he had four sound anchors holding him away from the reef, which was more than could be said then of any other ship in Apia harbor except *Calliope*.

Anxious watchers stood on the shore this night, unaware of the full extent of the tragedy before them. They could not see the changes in position of the ships, all of them dragging backward toward the Shore Reef, the three German ships and the *Nipsic* yawing dangerously near to one another as well as to the coral.

After midnight the three consuls had each gone to the beach, taking shelter behind sheds, shielding their faces with pieces of board. They could not stay long at the edge of the beach in those early hours; a man could scarcely stand unaided, so they went away, but soon they returned to the shore to wait and strain their eyes in the darkness.

The Samoans were first to sense that this storm would result in awful destruction to the ships in harbor. A messenger set out for Mataafa's camp before daybreak, taking the word of the catastrophe; when the messenger found Mataafa, in his sheltered house behind Matautu, the king did not ask whether the danger was to Americans or English or Germans; he called his chiefs and ordered 300 men to the beach, to see what they could do to help the foreign sailors.

As dawn broke over Apia and its harbor, the howling of the northerly winds among the trees and the crash of falling roofs brought scores of Apians from their beds. Through the blinding rain dozens of windswept figures could be seen congregating in the street, looking for spots where they could see into the harbor but remain sheltered from the tempest.

The tide was approaching full, and the waves washed over the single street of the town, taking out the roadway and splattering the debris with dark, dirty sand from the bottom of the anchorage. The spray was tossed like handfuls of rice at a wedding; the rain fell and was whipped by the wind into faces with the cutting force of sleet.

Until dawn, all that could be seen from shore was an occasional light; all that could be heard above the roar of the storm was fragmentary shouting from the officers and men aboard the ships. No sense could be made of what was heard, and virtually no movement could be seen; but at dawn's light, as the gray of sky lessened and the shapes of ships arose in contrast against the surging gray of the sea, the appalling situation of the ships became apparent to those on shore.

In the dim light foreigners and Samoans began picking their ways to the beach areas between the German Naval Hospital and the American consulate, for from this point they could gain their greatest vantage; the ships were slowly moving back to this corner of the harbor as though being forced into the neck of a funnel. The people ashore had to hold to each other for support, taking care not to trip and fall in the washed-out roadway. Here and there along the road they stepped across the trunks of coconut palms, reduced to little more than long serrated sticks, knobbed at one end where the fronds had blown away, straggling rootily at the other, where the earth had been washed from their bases.

Of the lovely orange grove that had stood a few hours earlier near the American consulate there was no recognizable sign. Not a piece of fruit was left on the tree; half the leaves were torn away, the very limbs and trunks shattered and twisted.

Among those who picked their way to the beach was the German *Doktor* Dierich, who had been shaken from his bed by the clattering of his windows, the trembling of the foundation of his house, and the shuddering of the walls.

Another who came in awe and worry was young Consul

Blacklock, and when he saw the tumultuous, charging sea and the bobbing ships, he realized more quickly than any man aboard any ship that the men-of-war were helpless in the storm. He turned and rushed back to the consulate to bring to the beach Lieutenant Fillette and the Marine guard.

Still another was *Lieutenant zur See* Burchard of the *Olga;* wounded in the battle of Vailele plantation, Lieutenant Burchard was scarcely recovered yet, but he could not keep from going to the shore to see what was happening to his ship and the others.

As Burchard neared the water, what he saw appalled him.

Across the foaming sea in the gathering dawn, it seemed that the ships were crossing and recrossing one another. Naturally, Burchard's eye sought his own ship *Olga* first, straining past *Eber* and *Nipsic* and beyond *Adler,* and he could make out her battered spars and see the broken shaft to the mizzen yard hanging askew on its mast. With rain-flecked glasses he swept the harbor and could read a small part of the tragedy in the broken masts and battered hulls.

Black smoke was pouring from every funnel. Funnels were all Burchard could see of *Trenton* and *Vandalia,* out still as they were on the edge of the anchorage. The smoke streamed out, almost at right angles to the funnels; then, as a lull came between gusts, the smoke shot up in clouds, only to be stripped away again by fresh wind. The force of the wind was now 12, dropping occasionally to Force 8, with eddies and whirlpools of wind and occasional breathing spaces, followed by splashing squalls. Only the *Nipsic*'s funnel could not be seen from shore, because that stack had become a dangerous weapon of destruction, rolling about the main deck of the gunboat, bending davits and smashing rails. The *Nipsic,* therefore, was wreathed in smoke aft of her foremast, and from the shore Burchard could see occasional streaks of flame, apparently arising out of her decks, and giving her the appearance of being afire. But desperate as was the condition of *Nipsic*, Lieutenant Burchard could tell that one ship was in worse straits. It was little *Eber*, closest in to shore, closest to the reef.

Eber's narrow escape from disaster to her propeller had come near the end of the middle watch, but at four o'clock in the morning when that watch ended, it made absolutely no difference to the men of the gunboat. Every man was at his action station, and *Kapitänlieutenant* Wallis kept the bridge, although theoretically young Sublieutenant Goedeke had the deck.

With the changing of the watch, *Obermaschinist* Teuber came on deck to discuss the problems he faced below: the propeller was working irregularly, he said.

Captain Wallis knew that he was not getting full power every time he needed it; the ship was slipping, and he could feel it.

It was not the engines, said Engineer Teuber, there was nothing wrong with the engines. In the encounter with the torque force of the anchor chain the propeller's fastenings must have loosened, and the propeller was slipping on the drive shaft.

As if that were not enough, Engineer Teuber added, as the propeller turned, he could feel its vibrations below, far more strongly than they could be felt on the pitching deck. The bent blade of the propeller could break at any moment, he said.

At least this bad news was offset by good: the pumps were working beautifully, First Officer Eckardt reported. *Eber* was taking a tremendous beating from the seas that washed over her decks, and the seawater was finding its way below, but there was not the slightest danger at this time from water in her.

Below, the galley crew was trying to keep the ship's cooking fires going and do something to prepare food for the men of the *Eber*. The crew had not eaten a meal since lunch the day before, and that meal had been a light one, with many men ashore and others off duty. *Oberbackersgaft* Wehner had baked bread early on the morning of March 15th, for supper that night, and practically none of it had been consumed. There was no chance to put a hot meal on the table—no table aboard the *Eber* could hold dish or glass in this storm—but Baker Wehner could slice some bread (lashing himself to his cutting block), and his helpers could spread the bread with gobs of lard so the men might have something to quiet the aches in their guts. It was not a meal, but it was food. *Kommandanten-Kellner* Kluge had an even more appropriate idea: he strained over the rocking, shifting stovetops and managed to heat enough water to make a steaming rum grog for the officers and the men on deck. With tankards and a chainful of tin cups over his shoulder, Kluge set out for the upper deck to reach the command bridge and then the waist and forecastle, followed by his helpers. Before Wehner and his assistant could lift their trays of bread up the companion-way, they were swamped, and the bread was drenched in seawater. As Kluge and his men stepped on deck, the waves broke over their heads, the tankards were engulfed, and by the time Kluge struggled, gasping, to the bridge, the grog he offered Captain Wallis was cold and salty.

The men were tossed about on the deck like stickmen. Every few minutes another seaman was forced below to Dr. Wachenhauer's sickbay for treatment—a bleeding cut if the man was lucky, a broken head or leg or arm if he was not.

On the beach Lieutenant Burchard watched, red-eyed and gasping from the force of the wind and rain. He wondered then how long *Eber* could take such a beating; the storm seemed to be worse where she lay, close inshore, than farther out, probably because of the whirlpools and crosscurrents caused by the rushing waters of the Vaisingano. Soon, not noticing the coming, Burchard was joined in his watching place by Manager Haidlen of the Vailele plantation. They exchanged a brief greeting and a nod—they had no energy for more, for both men's eyes were fixed on the scene before them, both squinted into the wind and stared out to sea. Watching little *Eber*'s smoke, they could tell that her engines were running full, and yet as they watched she drifted discernibly closer to the reef.

In the growing daylight, an exhausted Captain Wallis could see only too well his predicament, yet what could he do but pray? The wind was too stiff to mount canvas; a man climbing the rigging took his life in his hands, and he needed both of them—there was no hand for the ship in this hurricane. *Eber*'s engines were pounding, but Captain Wallis could feel the slippage of the propeller. An hour earlier it might have been giving him half-power, now it could not be pushing at more than a quarter of its old strength.

All Captain Wallis could hope for, numbly, all the men of the *Eber* could pray for, was that their one remaining starboard anchor would hold on the slippery coral.

As if to answer a prayer, the slow, steady dragging of the anchor ceased, that single anchor caught in some underwater obstruction, and it held fast, with *Eber*'s stern not twenty-five feet from the reef. The inbound tide pulled the ship, and the wind drove her, and Captain Wallis could feel the gunboat come up hard against her anchor—and *hold*. She pitched more sharply. As the surging seas rolled over her, she buried her bow a good six feet beneath the surface, and tons of water streamed across the decks, bowling over every man who was not fixed tight.

Captain Wallis headed the *Eber* ahead, trying to take off some of the strain; the riptide brought her back, slackening the chain, and then the storm had *Eber* in its grinding teeth again, and the forlorn, battered propeller's efforts could scarcely be noticed. Back *Eber* came, with a wrenching jolt as the anchor chain smacked against the hawseholes and strained. No chain could stand much more than this one had already; the anchor must slip, the chain must break, or the storm must somehow die.

The Captain saw his peril. Knowing now that his propeller was little more than a toy, he played it carefully, using his power in the rip and when the wind died off for a moment, judging, watching, waiting, calculating those brief moments when a little push would help his ship. He was not moving away from the reef—he could not hope for so much—but at least he seemed to be holding his own. If the anchor held, if the chain did not break . . .

In the gathering light after five o'clock, the people ashore watched this drama; their eyes were focused on it, for *Eber* was closest to them, closest to the reef; the other ships were waiting in the wings for their frightening performances.

Suddenly, aship and ashore, the drama of the *Eber* quickened; ashore the crowd could see, and aship the men could feel, a sinking, emptying loss; the anchor slipped. Actually, the anchor broke, one of its arms splitting off from the shank, fluke and all, and *Eber* was left with half an anchor to battle the fury of the storm.

The *Eber* began to drift, and she had not far to go. Desperately Captain Wallis signaled for full ahead, the propeller caught, the little ship shuddered for a moment as she headed into a tremendous sea—and the propeller failed! The engines churned, but there was no response from the shaft.

The *Eber* drifted rapidly. She was fifteen feet from the reef, ten feet, five feet—and then she was upon it, swinging broadside to, her port beam touching the coral so gently that the men could feel the impact: a grinding, but not a shock, a bump, a feeling of finality, but not a hurtful one.

Then a wave caught the little gunboat, a wave Lieutenant Burchard was prepared to swear was greater than any that had ever gone before. The little ship struck with a crash that could be heard on the beach, above the howl of wind and rain, but the ship came off, and for a moment her stern swung around, giving the spectators on the shore a view of the long gash that had been torn in her wooden side. And then another sea came crashing, nearly as strong as the first, and little *Eber* put her bow to the reef and plunged ahead.

For a moment *Eber* stood on her head, foredeck under a wave, useless screw gleaming high out of the water so the watchers could see how bent and battered it was. *Eber*'s bow bobbed, and she stood on her stern for a moment, then slid down along the side of the reef, gurgling, until she was seen no more.

Ashore, Lieutenant Burchard and Manager Haidlen stood stock-still as if paralyzed. One moment *Eber* was there, tossing on the water, little black shadows of men clutching her lines and fittings for survival. The next moment she was gone, and the wave that swept across the spot where she disappeared gave no hint of any touch of humanity beneath its gray-black base and foaming surface. All, all gone? Sturdy Captain Wallis? Dependable First Officer Eckardt? Brilliant navigator Lieutenant von Ernsthausen, so bright a future before him? Babyish, pale, slender, *Unterlieutenant* Gaedeke? Worldly surgeon Wachenhauer, who had spent so many off-duty hours at the bedsides of wounded men in the Naval Hospital? Paymaster Kunze? Engineer Teubel? And seventy men, skilled, brave fighting men? All gone, so close to land that any swimmer could have made it to shore in ten minutes on another day, and a well-manned longboat could halve that time?

Lieutenant Burchard stared until his eyes ached and smarted. All gone. There was nothing to be seen, nothing at all, save the flying scud and vicious green belly of the sea beneath it.

The Lieutenant saw nothing.

Nothing.

But then, what was that? It was a hand—no, it was a head, no, it was a back—it was all three—it was a man, rolling, tumbling, clutching upward at life as the sea brought him along the edge of the reef and in to shore.

Lieutenant Burchard and landsman Haidlen rushed to the water's edge, past the edge, into the water, up to their knees. They could not go farther, for at knee depth they could feel the sand giving way beneath their feet and the undertow pulling at their legs, even as the waves came crashing at them.

With a shout, down from the shore came a band of half a dozen Samoans, Mataafa's men, every one of them, sworn enemies of the Germans, but for all that, they came on, into the surf to help their enemies in the battle against the cruel sea.

Yes, there was a man, and as he tumbled shoreward in the water, Burchard and Haidlen grasped him by arm and legs, and the Samoans held them all fast so they would not be swept out by the undertow.

Then there was another man, and another, and another.

They came rolling, tumbling in, sputtering and dazed, swimming, perhaps, but their swimming was not saving them, they were being saved by the mercy of the storm, which offered back to life these pitiful few men of the crew of His Germanic Majesty's Ship *Eber*.

The four were pulled from the water, the best of them only half-conscious, cold and shaking, and they were bundled off by the Samoans and taken to the nearest building, the American consulate, where they were soon stripped and rubbed and blanketed and dosed with hot soup and whisky.

So four men were saved, among them Bo'sun Krause, who

had been on the bridge at his helmsman's post at the moment when the *Eber* struck. The four, plus four men of the *Eber* who had been ashore on guard duty or in hospital, were all that remained of the crew, all who could tell the story at home in Germany of the *Eber* and her adventures in the war.

An hour went by, and all that was to appear on the beach to signify that *Eber* had ever lived was a piece of her poor, shattered bowsprit that washed up at Lieutenant Burchard's feet.

Hope was quite given up for the crew of the *Eber,* and the attention of the watchers on shore was focused on other desperate men aboard other struggling ships, when Lieutenant Fillette happened to see a pale object sticking out beside a piling of the wharf between the German Hospital and the Evangelical Church. He hurried back from the beach, and under the wharf he found the half-conscious *Unterlieutenant* Gaedeke in water up to his chest, clinging to the piling.

Lieutenant Fillette pulled the German officer from under the wharf, and helped by others, he half-carried the youngster to the American consulate. It was an hour before any sense could be gotten out of Gaedeke. It had happened so fast, he said: he had been on the bridge with Captain Wallis, the other officers were at their stations below, the ship had gone down; no one had a chance to move five feet from his station. He did not know what had happened to Captain Wallis, but the others never had a chance.

CHAPTER TEN

Day of Death—7 a.m.

THE TWO great waves that smashed and sank the poor *Eber* were felt everywhere in the harbor and far beyond. On the southern coast the tidal waves struck Mua and flooded the land; already the wind had torn up more than five hundred coconut palms there, and had blown the roof off the great stone church; the tidal waves completed the damage. On the north shore of Upolu at Faleata bay the Samoans had gone to sleep in safety; they awoke just after five o'clock to the sound of the roaring wave; the first wave put several inches of water into the bottoms of their bamboo houses, and the second washed their canoes and boats up high on shore, next to the houses. The high-water mark was three feet above the highest tide known, and the Samoans were lucky that it came just after dawn at half-tide; had the tidal waves struck atop the full tide, the entire north shore of the island might have been laid waste and many lives lost to the angry sea.

Two days before the storm The Old Firm's schooner *Uvea* had left for Wallis Island, but she had tarried in Tutuila, so she was caught in midocean by the fury of the wind and forced into the shelter of a small island near Tutuila, where the shock of these two great waves and the wind dismasted her and left her a staggering hulk, barely afloat.

The great storm had reached hurricane force in Apia harbor before dawn, and it continued to increase in intensity this morning of March 16th. The storm was recurving, moving west and northwest from the southern point where it had encountered the *Altcar* storm (named for the British bark which reported it), and as the storm had recurved, looped north of Savaii Island, it doubled back on Upolu to bring its huge, devasting waves.

Aboard the *Trenton* Admiral Kimberly began, for the first time, to have doubts about the ability of the squadron to ride out the storm. He had never expected a hurricane this late in the season; he had never expected that with *Trenton*'s hamper down, and her hatches tightly battened, the flagship would be taking water, yet that was exactly what was happening. The bilge pumps in the engine room were all put on and the hand pumps were manned, yet as the light grew brighter with the coming of the day, the Admiral and Captain Farquhar could see for themselves what a beating the ship was taking, topside, and from below they learned from Lieutenant Commander Lyon, the First Officer, that the sea was gaining on the pumps and pumpers.

Lyon came to the bridge to consult with Captain Farquhar. As the Captain suspected, the greater part of the water was coming in through the hawsepipes, splashing onto the berth deck, and rising above the coamings, plunging through the hatches into the engine room. Everywhere below, the men were standing ankle-deep in water, and the water was rising.

At 5:45 when the first huge wave battered *Eber* against the Shore Reef's sharp side, that same wave drove the mattresses and blankets from the hawsepipes of *Trenton* and sent a stream of water into the engine room. Lieutenant Commander Lyon came to the bridge again. He wanted the

Captain's permission to stuff bedding into the hawsepipes, to cover the anchor chains and veer them into the hawsepipes to fill them up and keep the water out. Otherwise, he said, there was a very grave danger that the water would gain so far on them that the *Trenton*'s fire would be put out.

Captain Farquhar listened and nodded. Of course Mr. Lyon could follow this course. Let him try it and report in half an hour on its efficacy.

Aboard the *Vandalia,* tragedy struck at dawn. Captain Schoonmaker had left the bridge for an hour or so of rest and had gone down to his cabin before daybreak, secure in his trust that Lieutenant Carlin was in every way capable of handling any problem that might arise. He left the usual standing order that in case of emergency or visible worsening of the ship's situation, he was to be called immediately.

When the first great wave struck, John Myers, an oiler, was on the topgallant forecastle, and he was tossed aft in a swirl of water, bringing up with a crash against the cabin bulkhead, dazed and frightened, but only bruised. That wave was felt in the engine room as a tremendous shock—so strong that Engineer Webster first believed the ship had struck. But before the thought could more than flash through his mind, an immense mass of water came pouring through the engine-room hatch, knocking him from his perch on the upper platform and throwing him onto the moving machinery below. The great wave had boarded the ship forward and swept aft with nearly irresistible force, filling the decks hatch-high with water, drowning out the cabin, and throwing every man on deck off his feet.

Real tragedy occurred in the Captain's cabin. Captain Schoonmaker had just fallen asleep when the wave came. The impact threw him out of his bunk, across the cabin, and into a chair, head first. He struck so hard that his left ear was nearly torn from his head, and then he lay unconscious in the water on the deck for a moment, arousing just in time to take the shock of the second wave and strike his head again, gashing it in a different place. He lay on the floor, half-conscious, suffering from concussion and losing blood from his two gashes, until discovered by a seaman come to report from Lieutenant Carlin. Surgeon H. P. Harvey was summoned, and he made his tortuous way through the slippery companionways to the Captain's cabin to bind up his wounds. Hardly had the Captain come on deck, against the surgeon's advice, looking pale and ghastly, when again the ship gave a vicious lurch and Captain Schoonmaker was catapulted across the bridge to strike his head a third time on a spoke of the wheel. Quickly he was taken below to the wardroom, and Paymaster Arms and several other officers stayed with him to watch over his recovery from the blows. So heavy were the seas, and so all-pervasive, that the wardroom was nearly a foot deep in water from the moment the first tidal wave struck, and in spite of hand-bailing and the rigging of the handy billy, a portable force pump, the water came in as quickly as it was expelled.

As dawn came to Her Majesty's Ship *Calliope*, Captain Kane was dismayed to discover that in spite of his fine anchors the ship had dragged farther than he believed possible. Like all the inshore vessels, *Calliope* was very much in danger of being fixed on the reef and sunk.

At 5:30 Lieutenant McAlpine reported the stern hawser and sheet anchor were dangerously near the ship's screw and might foul it at any moment, so the Captain decided to sacrifice one of his precious anchors and told his First Lieutenant to cut the hawser. In a moment McAlpine and his damage control crew moved aft with fire axes to do the Captain's bidding.

Captain Kane then sent for Chief Engineer Bourke and told him to get steam up on all boilers for the first time.

Signaling full ahead, he steamed as far northeast as possible and then let go another sheet anchor, hoping to stop the dragging, unaware that the swift current of the Vaisingano had already done its work on the bottom of the harbor. "Full speed ahead" meant very little; the *Calliope* strained into the wind, but gathered way just in time to clear the reef after the kedge was dropped.

Swiftly the British ship's crew set to work to batten down against the storm, seeing in the daylight how much more serious it had become than the Captain or anyone else might have expected. The spare wheel-ropes were rove and manned, and so were the relieving tackles. Ten men were assigned to the great ship's wheel on the bridge, and half the watch was put to work straining at the relieving tackles.

Captain Kane could see *Vandalia* dragging down on top of his ship, getting closer every few minutes as her anchor chains slacked, then tightened, and slacked again, and the anchors slipped with each tightening, skidding across the hard coral. *Vandalia* was now ahead of *Calliope,* having drifted so far inshore; *Olga* stood off the British ship's starboard quarter; and the sharp reef stood off the port quarter, far too close.

At 5:30 the seas were coming over the topgallant forecastle and *Calliope,* too, was having trouble with her hawsepipes. The water surged through the pipes, filling the upper deck. But at least it was the *upper* deck on the *Calliope,* and although the decks were awash, the water was scuppered off and did not threaten the fires in the engine room.

At 5:45 the first tidal wave struck *Calliope,* carrying away the first cutter, the dinghy, the skiff, and the punt. The davits of all these were bent and battered and useless. This wave smothered the ship, making its way into every crevice and pushing below. In a moment the ship's hands were battening down, and the second wave was shunted off abovedecks, without serious damage to the engine room. But that second wave took its toll: a carpenter's mate was washed off his legs while battening down a hatchway, the surge smashed him against a shot rack, and he fractured his skull and lay unconscious until his mates could pick him up and take him below to Staff Surgeon Valentine Duke.

When the first tidal wave struck *Olga*, it buried her decks under tons of foaming brine, as it had those other ships, but she shook off the sea and came bow up, streaming spray into the wind. Two more guns were washed overboard from the damaged section of the port side of the ship where *Adler* had smashed through her timbers an hour earlier. From the poop, where he had stationed himself, Captain von Erhardt caught a glimpse of *Adler* as she porpoised in the heavy wave: the smaller ship had been carried completely around from *Olga*'s port, astern, to her starboard, and courtesy of the wave, her position relative to the reef was somewhat improved.

But *Adler* was still far too close to *Olga*, and as if to illustrate the danger, she rushed forward in the ebb of the great tidal wave and struck *Olga* again, this time on the starboard quarter. Impatiently, Captain von Erhardt called for a report on the damage, and First Officer Jaeckel again sped to comply. Fortunately, there was no major damage; the blow had been light, and no boats or guns or vital tackle had been lost.

On the shore, Mataafa's three hundred Samoan warriors had arrived from Matautu and were clustered in the area around the American consulate, watching the desperate battle of the ships with the sea and wind. They were led by Chief Salu Ana, aide to Mataafa himself, and they had been joined by Chief Seumanu Tafa, of the Apia district, who had brought his own trusted followers and canoes to the shore. The canoes were useless at the moment; there was no hope for so frail a craft in the raging waters; so fast was the current going out from shore at the mouth of the Vaisingano that it was clocked at 6 knots by one of the naval officers, and that was only the surface current. Earlier in the night, when the *Lily* had gone down, trader Anthony Ormsby and the Hawaiian mate had been swept by that current out past the *Olga,* past the *Calliope* and *Vandalia,* whose crews had thrown out life rings to no avail, out beyond the jutting arms of the reef to the open sea. A canoe or a swimmer might be caught in the current or in the undertow, or dashed against the reef and thrown to the bottom and whisked beyond the harbor. Already the bodies of the German sailors of the *Eber* were being carried outside, and some of them would be cast up as far off as five miles from the harbor.

It was not time for action from the shore, for there was nothing to be done to save ships or men: they must save themselves, or go down.

In the still-gathering wind and rain of the storm, the eyes of the watchers on the shore were turned to the *Nipsic,* for she was in sore trouble.

After the smokestack had been felled, the ton and a half of metal went careening across the deck with every motion of the ship, striking terror into the hearts of the crew. Some men were sure the ship was burning, and the billowing black smoke that bit into their eyes and noses brought more panic.

Captain Mullan ordered the stack belayed, but he was not heard. Half the crew had run up the rigging and hung there, refusing to return to duty, panic-stricken, some of them paralyzed with fear. Within five minutes of the blow that brought down the iron stack, the *Nipsic* was totally demoralized; only her officers and a handful of enlisted men would make a move to try to save the ship. As for the rest, they had turned into a faceless mob, useless to the ship and dangerous to themselves.

When the first tidal wave struck, three of the panic-stricken men were swept overboard; as their mates saw them go, the panic increased, and more crewmen leaped into the rigging, holding on with arms and legs, refusing to obey the orders of their officers.

The officers were disgusted and furious with the cowards of the crew. But not all the men rebelled in their fear. Ensign H. P. Jones was officer of the deck, and he stood on the bridge, superintending the steering, to keep the *Olga* off; the smoke blinded him, the heat from the open fires seared up the broken stack and flashed across the deck at eye level, and half the time he could see only a few feet; yet he stood, rocklike, next to his captain. And beside him, at the conn, was Quartermaster R. H. Taylor, who never once faltered in the heat and smoke and soot, drenched as he was by wave and spindrift. Seamen James Lane and Henry Ponseel fought bravely with the big wheel; even when the *Olga* struck twice and it seemed certain the *Nipsic* would go down, they did not flinch or turn away.

Chief Boatswain's Mate John Bradley rushed up and down the decks, cursing the men in the rigging and shaking his fist at them; he and Boatswain's Mate William Cosgrove pulled together the men who were in command of their senses and took them to Lieutenant Hawley, executive officer of the *Nipsic,* who was striving earnestly to repair the damage on deck and batten the ship down so she would stop taking water below.

When the second tidal wave struck the *Nipsic,* the water rushed into the engine room through the broken stack and ventilators, half-extinguishing the fires and dousing what little draft remained.

Wet coal was not enough. Chief Engineer George Hall reported to Captain Mullan that he could not keep up the fires, but the *Nipsic* was barely holding her own against the tide and sea with three anchors out, her chains paid out full, and the one chance of salvation lay in keeping up steam, keeping the engines going and the propeller turning. Captain Mullan ordered the Chief Engineer to begin breaking up woodwork and any other burnables, and the black gang turned to the task, but the wood did not catch quickly enough or burn hot enough, and the battle was being lost, as quickly as it could be. Suddenly, Captain Mullan remembered the barrels of salt pork and the supply of hams from Chicago hanging in the ice rooms. Here was potential heat aplenty, and he sent Quartermaster Gunner Brooks Cason, his messenger, down to the engine room to tell the Chief Engineer to break into the ship's stores.

The three men who were washed overboard by the first great wave had not far to go; *Nipsic* was following the course of *Eber*. No longer did the bow of *Olga* threaten the American ship; she had moved far inshore, and the wind and sea were pushing her steadily toward the Shore Reef. The men overboard clutched and scrabbled at the water that closed over their heads and were borne on this tremendous wave inland, to wash up gasping, safe on the sands before the American consulate. Willing hands, Samoan and American, grasped them and carried them to the consulate, which had been turned into an infirmary in the past few hours.

Aboard the *Nipsic* Captain Mullan observed the gradual slippage of his three anchors, and not knowing that no metal would hold on that slippery, scoured coral sea bottom he determined to bring more weight to bear, to help the anchors hold the ship off the reef. By six o'clock the seas were breaking regularly over the ship, and tons of water cascaded down her decks as she pitched and yawed in trough and peak. The ship was making water faster than the pumps or bailers could free her, and Lieutenant Hawley needed help to try to save the steam in the boilers. The Captain ordered the lee gun-ports opened, and they were let down, so the water stream-ing down to the gun deck would drain off between lunges.

Lieutenant Hawley then turned his attention on to an attempt to relieve the hard-pressed anchors. The 8-inch gun on the *Nipsic's* forecastle was unshipped and attached to a hawser. Hawley intended to drop the gun to starboard and hoped to use it as a kedge, to gain back some of that precious chain that had been completely extended from the bowers.

The greatest immediate dangers to the ship were not the reef, but the plunging pipe that had been the *Nipsic's* smoke-stack and the *Olga,* which might bear down on the American ship once again. Quartermaster John Callahan had been stationed on the quarter since the middle watch to guard against *Olga,* and in spite of constant pounding from the seas and virtual exhaustion, he did not leave his post. Lieutenant John Shearman and a handful of men set out to tame the raging stack and ease the panic of the crew. They moved gingerly about the main deck where the stack was rolling, much as picadors move around a fresh bull in the ring, grant-ing all the caution a dangerous beast deserves. The stack rolled this way and that, smashing the second after ventilator and reducing it to rubbish. Had the stack fallen straight back, it might have rolled over the deck and off, past the broken port hammock rail, but no, it was athwartships, and it rolled back and forth between pilothouse and mainmast, threatening every man on the main deck. Finally, the work party managed to place a heavy block beneath the broken stack just as the ship pitched forward, then another aft, and then it was relatively simple to shore up the blocks with others and tie the monster down.

Captain Mullan had moved back to the poop deck, where he had a better command post than on the bridge forward of the mainmast, particularly after collisions with *Olga* had damaged the ship so severely amidships. The smoke and flame from the furnaces was so heavy on the bridge that the ship could not be conned from there.

Between 6:15 and 6:30 the officers made every attempt to calm the demoralized men and get them back to the effort of saving the ship. The salt pork and hams burned with a heavy, greasy smoke, but they did burn, and that was the important matter. The steam pressure, which had dropped dangerously, increased until there seemed to be more than a bare chance that *Nipsic* could survive and even move away from her dangerous position near the reef. Then, at 6:30, the ship took a heavy sea on the starboard bow, just as she moved ahead to relieve the port anchor. The starboard bower chain tightened, there was a sudden cracking sound, and the ship lurched heavily to port, then dragged backward, dangerously near the reef.

Captain Mullan heard the crack and knew what was happening almost before the ship began dragging. He was faced with a moment of decision: should he try to heave overboard the 60-pound rifle on the forecastle and consider that a substitute for his lost bower anchor? Could the engines make enough steam for him to ride out the storm, even with his damaged stack?

The problem was more complicated than that, even. The supply of salt pork and hams was running low, and when these highly combustible fuels were gone, what would he use to feed the flames? No low-grade fuel, not even coal, would hold in the furnaces without the usual draft.

Then, too, there was the question of his crew: the seamen were practically useless, mutinous; half the men would not answer a simple order, but clung to the rigging for their very lives; and how much longer could he count on the black gang?

Mullan called for Chief Engineer Hall and asked for his opinion. At best, the engineer said, the fires were weakening, and if the rain and storm continued, no one could tell how long they might last.

The decision, as always, was the Captain's.

The ship was yawing very heavily from north-northeast to north, and the port anchor was not holding. They had come more than halfway across the harbor and were pushing toward the point where the *Eber* had struck an hour before. The wind was blowing a gale, variable in direction, ranging from Force 8 to 12. *Nipsic* had used five tons of coal in the past twenty-four hours, and she had another 75 tons aboard, but coal was of no use to her now and would not save her. The hatches were all battened down, except for the forecastle hatch, but she was taking water; there was four inches of water in the magazine, and water had been coming in the wardroom hatch, so that the three ship's chronometers were wrecked and so was the comparing watch; and the deck seams were opening on the quarterdeck, which meant the ship would soon begin taking more water, when every drop threatened her weakened fires.

Faced with a useless crew, a hurricane that seemed to grow worse hour by hour, rather than better, and a battered ship whose power plant was threatened, Captain Mullan decided to try to beach *Nipsic* to save the ship, perhaps, but at least to save the men.

Nipsic was heading north-northeast into the teeth of the wind, perhaps fifty yards separating the reef from her port quarter. The problem would be to cast loose the port bower, the sheet anchor, and turn her strongly enough and quickly enough to starboard to get around before the sea caught her by the beam and smashed her against the reef. At 6:40 the prisoners were released from the brig, and as soon as Captain Mullan had the word, Lieutenant Hawley was told of the plan to slip the port bower, while another gang would chop away the hawser fixed to the sheet anchor riding astern.

Ensign Jones stood at the Captain's side, to relay orders. The moment the anchors were slipped was critical; the ship must have every bit of steam she could manage. Below, Engineer Hall crammed the furnaces with the pork and used every trick he knew to stir a draft, but he could not get the steam pressure to rise.

It was now or never, for Captain Mullan. Resolutely stern, more than determined, the Captain issued his orders.

"Full speed ahead."

The engine telegraph clanked and clanked again to deliver and confirm the order.

"Stand by to slip port bower chain."

Ensign Jones relayed the order, and it was carried down the deck by a succession of messengers, only a few feet apart, bawling the words so they might be heard forward.

The ship responded, giving Captain Mullan a bit more than he had hoped for.

"Stand by to cut hawser."

Ensign Jones turned and relayed the message aft.

With one last look over his left shoulder at the sea boiling on the edge of the Shore Reef, now perhaps thirty yards away, the Captain said the words.

"Slip port bower. Cut hawser. Hard astarboard, full rudder."

The port bower chain, veered to its fullest, was suddenly released, and splashing once, the chain disappeared beneath the green-white foam. Two chops with the fire axes at the taffrail, and the sheet anchor hawser parted, the loose end snaking across the waves as the anchor pulled it back and below.

"Hard aport!" the Captain shouted, raising his voice for the first time. "Ninety degrees, full rudder."

Captain Mullan had chosen his moment and his maneuver well. Pushed by the sea, her engines roaring, *Nipsic* had swung to starboard, and the wind hurried her along, aimed as she was at the narrow strip of beach between the southeast edge of the Shore Reef and the southwest bank of the Vaisingano, perhaps a hundred yards away. As her bow swung around toward the beach, the wind caught the ship and threatened to take her broadside, catch her on the starboard quarter, slew her around, and toss her on the reef, but by her swing to port, the wind was brought off the port quarter and the glancing force of it helped her on her way to shore, pulling her away from the reef rather than into it, and keeping her starboard in the lee.

Never had *Nipsic* traveled a hundred yards so quickly. With a gentle shudder she struck the soft sand. As she came in, the engineers and terrified black gang rushed up from below, not slowing to bank the fires or even to stop the engines. She struck, she quivered, and her engines continued to drive her, screw in the water and then out of it, racing, slowing, racing, giving an uncertain rhythm to all that went on abovedecks.

As the ship hit sand, the Captain ordered Surgeon Ezra Derr and half a dozen sick and injured men into the first cutter, and a crew to take them in to shore, now only a few short yards away from the bow of the *Nipsic*. The starboard boats were on the lee, and the cutter was launched without incident. But at it swung away from the ship, even protected by the hull, the boat capsized, and Surgeon Derr, his injured and infirm men, and the oarsmen were thrown into the raging surf to swim and crawl and struggle those few yards to safety, or to drown.

Seeing their predicament, Lieutenant Richard Davenport, the navigator, leaped into the sea from the forecastle and struck out for shore himself. When this officer abandoned ship, so did a half-dozen of the more terrified seamen, and all swam in safely.

After the damage done by the *Olga,* there were not enough boats left aboard *Nipsic* to bring all the men ashore, even had the crew been under control, had the seas not been smashing into and over the port side. A look over the side showed Captain Mullan that it was nearly suicidal for men to try to swim for shore except from the bow. Ahead he could see the struggling boat's crew in the water—and they had been halfway to safety before one huge wave swamped their cockleshell.

The Captain called for volunteers to man the gig and carry a line to shore.

From the shore, Mataafa's men, led by Seumanu Tafa, came rushing to the water's edge as *Nipsic* beached. When the doctor's cutter capsized, the Samoans formed a human chain, with the men farthest out standing waist-deep in the charging surf as it ebbed and pulled at them, water splashing over their heads as the waves came in. Buoyed by their oarsmen, the sick half-floated, half-swam the few yards remaining, and every man was saved by the glad grasping hands of the Samoans, who passed them man to man back to the safety of the beach, where they were allowed to collapse, gasping but alive, on the wet sand. Surgeon Derr was nearly drowned; he was being carried out to sea when Charles Freuen, a native of Apia, leaped into the surf and rescued the doctor.

Seeing the first swimmers saved, two frightened members of the black gang leaped overboard amidships and struck out for shore. They had not looked before they leaped. What had saved the men of the doctor's boat and the first who panicked was a crescent sandbar, 150 yards long and 40 feet wide, which had been thrown up by the current of the Vaisingano outside the entrance, forming a sort of lagoon around the mouth of the river. Halfway inshore from the *Nipsic,* the influence of the sandbar kept the current of the river from dragging at the swimmers in the capsized cutter. But where the *Nipsic* lay there was no such protection, and the two swimmers must contend with the inshore pressure of the surf, but also with the ebb of the undertow and the 6-knot seaward current of the Vaisingano. The two dived into a mountainous sea and surfaced, then struck out for shore, but immediately those ashore and on the ship could see that the swimmers were in trouble. The first to leap had been a coal-heaver, David Patrick Kelleher. He took a stroke, then sank, came up gasping, sinking and clawing, and disappeared. The second swimmer, First Class Fireman William Watson, struck out for shore bravely enough, but the current of the river or the ebb tide caught him and dragged him under, and the next that anyone saw of Watson, his head appeared just once, twenty yards on the *weather* side of the *Nipsic*, moving rapidly toward the center of the harbor and the open sea.

Then he, too, disappeared.

When the Captain called for volunteers to take the gig to shore, Coxswain Henry Pontseel at the wheel was the first man to step forward. Pontseel had been straining at the wheel since one o'clock in the morning without a break, yet he volunteered for this dangerous task.

The volunteers were few enough: John Gill, another seaman, Joshua Heap and George Callan, both *apprentices,* and Thomas Johnson, a lowly cabin steward.

Where were the able-bodied seamen, the petty officers, and the old Navy hands? Terrified, they were clinging to the rigging, demanding to be saved, but doing nothing to save themselves.

A light line was attached to a shot rail, and the coil was taken into the gig. The volunteers stepped into the boat, and other seamen lowered the boat in the davits. Suddenly the men on one end dropped the rope, and the gig went into the water on end, spilling the five volunteers into the sea. In a moment they were all swept back along the side of the *Nipsic* and away.

The mob that had been a ship's crew crowded onto the forecastle, from which it was so short a distance to the shore and safety. Below, on the beach, a hundred Samoans rushed as close to the bow of the vessel as they could come, and shouted and gestured to the men of the *Nipsic* to throw a line. In a few moments the Captain came to the bow, as well, and the search for a line began. One was found and it was weighted and cast with the following wind. It fell short of the shore, and a Samoan leaped into the water, swam for it, grasped it, and then, torn away, whipped around the side of *Nipsic* and disappeared.

Another attempt was made. This time no over-brave Samoan tried to swim through this deadly sea. The second cast fell short, but a cast did reach one human chain, and the Samoans soon had the line taut.

A double hawser was fixed to the line and dragged ashore through the surf. The Captain and his officers then elbowed the men aside, as the crewmen tried to scramble down the lines, and the officers brought some semblance of discipline back to the lost ship's crew.

Wind and sea were increasing even as the rescue efforts began. The surf pounded at the port quarter of the *Nipsic* so hard those aboard feared she would not last until they could get off. The whine of the screw could be heard, plaintive as a siren, as the propeller surged in and out of the waves.

Ashore, on one end of the line of rescuers Seumanu Tafa stood straight and proud, directing the rescue attempt. On the other end was Salu Ana, working with every bit as much will to bring the men away from the stricken vessel.

So terrible were the seas that the ebbing surf smashed against the stem of the *Nipsic* with so much force that watchers thought she would be driven off the sand and back against the reef; so great the wind that clouds of sand flew through the air from the bar above the *Nipsic,* blinding the rescuers; so great the undertow that the sure-footed Samoans must rope themselves together and catch one of their number as he was dragged away from them. The Samoans shouted and chanted as they pulled the hawsers and held them tight so the men of the *Nipsic* could scramble down.

Aboard the *Nipsic* it was all Captain Mullan could do to preserve order; had not the two terrified members of the black gang drowned before their very eyes, half the crew of the *Nipsic* would have leaped overboard; now they fought for position to be first to climb down to safety.

Ashore, Ensign J. L. Purcell, who had been in Apia on duty, came out waist-deep into the water to direct the rescue of the ship's crew. On board, Captain Mullan and the officers crowded at the rail and kept order, putting the sick over first. Ensign H. A. Field had been in sickbay, but had refused to go ashore. He was ordered ashore now, and went, but when he reached the bottom of the rope, he shook off his rescuers and went back into the surf to help others.

The sea was rolling in so fast and high beneath the bows of the *Nipsic* that before the men had moved down ten feet from the cutwater they were submerged, and only by wrapping arms and legs around the hawsers could they pull themselves to the point where the willing hands of the Samoans pried them loose.

In the fashion of sailors, a few had treasures or valuables tied up in handkerchiefs, and these men risked their lives to save their possessions and would not let go of them at any cost; but most of the crew of the *Nipsic* were in shirts and trousers, or even less (the sea had washed the clothes off some men's backs), and most had long before discarded shoes to gain a firmer grip on the wet deck with bare feet.

An hour went by, and then another. Nearly all Apia was now on the beach, braving the ferocious wind and rain to watch the rescue of the sailors. In time, the frightened men were moved ashore, and the air of panic on the deck of the *Nipsic* wore away.

As the seamen reached the line of waiting Samoans, half a dozen hands grasped each man and bore him gently to the American consulate, where Consul Blacklock and Surgeon Derr had set up an emergency aid station.

Lieutenant Fillette of the Marine guard had routed out a neighboring storekeeper and had requisitioned his supply of clothing, so that as each man from the *Nipsic* came ashore, shivering, he was whisked to the consulate, examined by the doctor and put to bed if he was hurt or exhausted, dried and given a suit of dry clothing if he was not. The halls and rooms of the consulate were crowded with lines of men sitting on the floors, backs against the walls, resting. Some, in little knots, sat around smoking and passing scuttlebutt, watching the doors to try to identify the new arrivals as they were brought inside.

On the deck of the *Nipsic,* Ensign Jones was among the last to go ashore, and he grasped the logbook of the ship to take with him on a journey made more perilous by this concern. Halfway down the hawser, a wave swept over him, and he could feel his grip slipping; he dropped the logbook, and the logs of March 12th, 13th, 14th, and 15th went to the bottom of the harbor.

Next came two brave sailors who had stayed so long to help the others, and finally Captain Mullan and Lieutenant Shearman were left alone on the deck.

The Captain could not swim and dreaded the thought of drowning. He insisted that he must have some kind of breeches buoy in which to make his way to safety, so Lieutenant Shearman found an empty water cask, which he attached to the hawser; Captain Mullan climbed into the cask, and the Lieutenant lowered him away to the waiting hands of the Samoans, then clambered down the hawser himself.

The last man was off the *Nipsic*. The deserted engines had stopped their drumming. The screw no longer turned. The seas broke high across her decks, tearing away the mainmast at the second band from the spar deck, carrying away the cutwater weakened by the pressure of so many bodies clambering over it, and, above all, smashing at the *Nipsic*'s sides and rolling her on her bottom. The rudder was washed back and forth with no one to control its sway, and soon the tackle broke, and the rudder, rudderpost, and shoe were carried away by the power of the sea. Part of the false keel was broken off; so was part of the sternpost. Yet *Nipsic* sat, firm aground, and took the storm alone.

CHAPTER ELEVEN

Day of Death — 8 a.m.

SINCE MIDNIGHT, the captains in Apia harbor had been waiting for the wind to shift around past north to north-northwest and to the west, which would mean the end of the blow, but instead the wind gauge moved to just east of north and stuck there. The winds continued to blow into Apia harbor at Force 12—72 miles an hour and more.

It was not a steady wind; it might have been better for the ships still afloat had it been steady, for at least then the men at the conn could estimate the probable actions of their ships. But the wind blew fitfully, sometimes as low as Force 7, then rising with a shriek back to hurricane force. By seven o'clock, when *Nipsic* went hard aground on the sand before the American consulate, it was apparent to the captains of the ships still afloat that they were far from finished with this storm. The wind was not shifting or dying, it was increasing gradually, and the waves and currents pitted against the puny men in their ships grew stronger by the hour.

One effect of the worsening hurricane was to set up a counterclockwise system of currents within the harbor. The waters of the Vaisingano rushed outward along the eastern reef to the edge of the harbor, the surf breaking over them and creating new riptides every minute. Along the western reef or Shore Reef, a strong current had developed, which tended to pull the ships inshore and aim them for the spot where *Eber* had gone down.

In his cabin aboard the *Trenton*, Admiral Kimberly tried to make some sense of the barometer and wind readings. Between midnight and four o'clock in the morning the barometer had risen from 29.36 to 29.38, then it had begun to drop again, falling to 29.23 by six o'clock. The wind, however, had steadily increased in force all night and during the early morning hours. The Admiral came to the unwelcome conclusion that this storm had been generated directly over Apia, that they were sitting next to the eye of the storm, that it was making no progressive movement, and that the worst was yet to come. If he was right (which he was not), then he could expect the barometer to continue to fluctuate, the winds to continue to blow around the circle, and the seas to continue to rise. Under the circumstances, it was as well that the Admiral kept this conclusion to himself.

Ashore, Consul Blacklock moved from his consulate to the beach, talking with the American officers and the Samoans who stood silently, looking outward at the ships struggling for survival. Consul de Coetlogon collected his family in the English consulate and knelt with them to pray for the Englishmen, Americans, and Germans out there, exposed to the full fury of the elements. Consul Knappe, on the Matautu side of the Vaisingano, found himself cut off from his consulate by the collapse of the shore-road bridge. The flood of the Vaisingano had carried a score of palm trees down the torrent, the trunks had battered furiously at the bridge supports, and before dawn the bridge had collapsed, one side completely swept away, a narrow railing and a few supports all that remained of the other. Consul Knappe and his helpers rigged ropes across the water on the old piers, and he inched his way tenuously across the flooded river to Matafele and the building of H. M. Ruge and Company, which he had taken over as temporary consulate after the big fire.

Soon Consul Knappe returned to the beach with the fifty German Marines and sailors who had been detailed to guard the consulate. They were stationed on the beach, an armed guard, to be sure the Samoans did not attack German sailors as they came ashore. Germany was at war with Samoa's Mataafa, and Consul Knappe acted within the framework of his experience and European mores; there was no reason for him to understand, and he did not think to ask, that to Samoans nature was the enemy, and for the moment at least there was no thought less noble in the minds of Seumanu Tafa and the others than to save every life that could be wrenched from the evil sea.

At seven o'clock Lieutenant Commander Lyon on the *Trenton* completed the battening down of all the hatches on the spar deck except the cabin hatch—the sea had become so much worse that *Trenton* was taking water that high. Suddenly, a huge sea swept around broadside against the *Trenton*'s rudder, breaking the rudderpost and unshipping the rudder itself. As the rudder was destroyed, the steering ropes dragged the big ship's wheel off its base, then parted like kitestring. The two helmsmen were thrown over the wheel, their legs were broken, and one of them suffered serious internal injuries.

Scarcely had the men been taken below when the starboard bridle port was stove in by the sea with such force that J. Hewlett, a Negro sailor standing near the port, was killed instantly.

Immediately the word was passed to the main deck, and not a second was lost, for every man knew that here disaster threatened the ship; the starboard bridle port was six feet long and four feet wide, the bow port on the gun deck; tons of water passed by that port every time the ship's bow dipped into a trough and the sea splashed over her decks; if the port could not be repaired, and quickly, *Trenton* was as good as lost.

The word was flashed along the deck.

Gunner Westfall was the first man to respond to the call. He shouted for volunteers and hastened forward from the main deck.

When Westfall reached the bow, he saw that he was none too soon, that the damage was as he had feared. As he came to the broken port, *Trenton* dropped her head and plunged, and an Atlantean wave rushed through the twenty-four square feet of opening, completely flooding the gun deck. Half a dozen torrents like that one would put out the ship's fires and leave *Trenton* helpless before the storm.

Gunner Westfall saw what must be done. He ordered men aft to bring up capstan bars and hammocks and mattresses. One capstan bar must be placed outside, and hooked with tackles inside, to hold the barricade that would be built to keep out the sea. Someone must go outside and strap the bar in place, hanging out of the port while he did so.

Gunner Westfall called for a volunteer.

There was no reply.

The men took one sidelong glance outside at the sea snarling below them so close and backed away.

There was no time to go back and seek other volunteers, no time to argue. Gunner Westfall picked up the capstan bar and straps.

"Well, I will go," he said, and he moved toward the shattered port.

The others tried to hold him back, but he shook them off. One man must risk his life, or all were as good as drowned, and he would rather take the immediate chance than wait for certainty.

He was no fool, this gunner, and he did not simply climb outside into the fury of the storm; he waited while *Trenton* took another dousing bath inside that port, and then, just as she brought her head up, he slipped outside, into the teeth of the howling wind, the men holding his legs, and he fixed the straps around the capstan bar and wedged it tight so it would not slip inside the broken port.

The wind tore at his fingers, and the salt spray tortured his eyes, and he was twice as long in adjusting the straps as he ought to have been; then it was done, and he nodded to his men to haul him back through the opening. They pulled his legs and back he came, not a moment too soon, for as they pulled, another sea came charging in the broken port, drenching everyone. Had Westfall been still outside, he would have been torn away from those who held him and carried away from the ship.

The preparations made, Westfall looked behind him and saw his men coming up with hammocks and mattresses. He sent another man aft to find a table, and when he returned, the mattresses were piled against the broken port, with hammocks stuffed around the cracks, the table was wedged against the mattresses, and the tackles were hooked behind the table.

Trenton began to dip her bow again. Now the men would see how well their barricade would hold.

The cutwater went down, the sea came up, and the men shoved against the table and the mattresses, but only for a moment; they were knocked off their feet, half their barricade of bedding was washed away, and the water came charging in.

Yet only half as much water had come in as came before, and discouraged as Gunner Westfall was, he would not let the men see, for he sensed that their will to struggle was leaving them and that if he faltered they would quit, and all would be lost.

Westfall grabbed another capstan bar and began ramming home the mattresses that the men slid in front of the table. Then came more stuffing—and then another wave. This time the result was better than before, and even the men could see progress, although after each wave they must pick themselves up off the deck.

Another wave, and another, and they were almost holding their own. As the men went down like ninepins on that fourth wave, Westfall jumped up and led a cheer—and the men moved with a new will back to the barricade.

Aboard the *Vandalia*, Lieutenant Carlin realized that he must take the full responsibility for the salvation of the ship, because Captain Schoonmaker was barely more than conscious. So busy was Carlin with the *Vandalia* that he had no time to pay attention to other ships, unless, like *Calliope*, they were so close as to threaten his own charge. *Calliope* he saw and saw very well, for she had slipped back until *Vandalia* was playing beneath the British ship's bows. It was almost fascinating to watch: *Calliope*'s bow rose up sixty feet on the crest of a wave, towering above the *Vandalia*, the British ship's undercut steel ram exposed menacingly. *Calliope*'s bottom would be exposed as far abaft as the mainmast, then, the crest past, the warship would smash down thunderingly, a few yards off *Vandalia*'s port quarter. From *Vandalia* the frightful impact of the steel ship on the sea gave warning of what might happen to the wooden American warship if the sea gods willed it.

When *Eber* went down, Lieutenant Carlin did not even know it for half an hour. When *Nipsic* beached, he was too busy to watch the desperate battle of her men against the surf and wind; he took the poop and sent Cadet Wiley, his messenger, forward with all messages that must be carried through the waist. The youngster was tiring. For nearly seven hours he had been scrabbling back and forth across the deck, fighting heavy seas on every trip, hanging onto the lifelines as he ran and crawled from one sheltered spot to the next.

Below, the engine room was flooded and had been since *Vandalia* was boarded by the first great tidal wave. Engineer Harrie Webster stripped down to shirt, trousers, and shoes and stood soaking on his upper platform, watching everything in the engineering department, with special attention to the steam gauge and the clinometer that measured the ship's angle as she pitched and yawed in the sea.

From time to time, Lieutenant Carlin appeared at the engine-room hatch, usually to ask for more steam in the boilers and to inquire anxiously about the condition of the power plant. Gradually, Engineer Webster increased the steam until it reached a pressure of 60 pounds, which was all he dared make, no matter what the deck crew ordered.

By daylight it had become necessary for every man to keep a grip on something as the ship lurched. The task of the coal-heavers was made a fantastic dance: heave, rush back and hold the handrail, wait for the shuddering impact of bow smashing into wave, snatch a shovel of coal, heave, rush back and hold, wait, smash, snatch, heave, rush. . . .

The sweat poured down their grimy faces in gray streaks, the water sloshed about their shoes, and the deck grew slippery. A man fell and cursed. Another man lurched into the furnace edge and burned his forearm, and the cursing was punctuated by hold, wait, smash, snatch, heave, rush, smash. . . .

From Engineer Webster's place on the upper platform only one set of facts existed, the facts of the engine room. The smell of grease, the hot breath of the engines and the furnaces, the whine of the shaft and the motors, the clanking of doors and the whoosh of fires, all these were as usual, augmented as they might be by the fear of the black gang and the rush of water down the hatch that drenched Engineer Webster from head to toe every few minutes and sent shivers of cold and fear down his spine.

But as to what went on in the outside world, Engineer Webster and the black gang learned only the news that was brought to them and flung down the open hatch. *Eber* was under, they learned at daybreak; *Adler* was drifting toward the same fate; *Nipsic* was aground.

At seven o'clock Engineer Webster was assured from above that the *Vandalia*'s anchors had not dragged and that if the engines held out, there need be no fear for the safety of the ship. If it was not quite a truthful statement, Lieutenant Carlin could be forgiven, because the life of every man in the ship depended on the performance of those below, and if they panicked, as had the black gang of the *Nipsic*, then *Vandalia* was surely lost.

The word passed at seven to Engineer Webster was not strictly true; *Vandalia* had slipped, her chains were veered full out, and minute by minute they were dragging, the anchors lessening their holding power as they moved toward each other, fathom by fathom.

By 7:30 it was apparent to Engineer Webster that this storm was like none he had ever experienced before. From his perch in the engine room the best that he could see on any normal day was a glimpse of sun and sky through the engine-room hatch, but by 7:30 on the morning of March 16th, the ship was rolling and careening so madly that the deck was almost perpendicular to the sea. On one of these mad rolls, Engineer Webster caught a glimpse of the *Calliope,* and he saw her keel standing almost over him.

He saw *Calliope* once, and he saw her again, almost on top of *Vandalia,* pitching and tossing like an eggshell. This

second time, as Engineer Webster held on to his guard railing and looked above and out, he also saw sailors rushing
madly forward past the engine-room hatch on deck, and then
he felt a fierce shock go through the ship: *Calliope* had struck
her. The ship shuddered, and for a moment Engineer
Webster thought the end had come. Every man in the engine
room was thrown to the deck. Then he saw *Calliope* again,
still plunging off the port quarter, and *Vandalia* seemed to
settle down.

Of all the ships in the harbor, *Olga*'s position was most
secure. She had drifted least of any, riding to her four anchors. She had no real fear of other warships after *Nipsic*
moved in to the beach, and Captain von Erhardt had the most
reason for optimism of any commander in the harbor.

Still fairly near the *Olga*, although slipping rapidly toward
the western reef's north spit, lay the *Adler*, lying far too
close down on the reef for comfort. She was about two hundred yards west of the point where *Eber* had struck and gone
under.

Just before seven o'clock, First Officer Arend and Navigator Caesar came to the bridge and asked Captain Fritze to
give up the hope of saving the ship and run her onto the
beach. Captain Fritze was most loath to do so, as long as he
felt there was a chance of saving the ship as well as the lives
of the men. Then the weather seemed to grow worse, and
as if to punctuate the growing power of the storm, from the
depths next to the reef came up bits of wreckage from the
Eber, clearly visible to the men of *Adler*.

By eight o'clock Captain Fritze saw that *Adler* was drifting
surely onto the Shore Reef. Only one anchor was left to
Captain Fritze by this time, and it was not holding; he
called *Obermaschinist* Goetze to the bridge and asked the
engine room to give every ounce of steam possible, because

he wanted to try to take the ship off the reef and out to sea. Poor *Adler!* With her underpowered engines, and suffering as she was from steering troubles, the chance was very slight that she could make it outside, but Captain Fritze was determined to try, and Goetze promised to do his best.

The engineer went back below. Captain Fritze glanced off to his port quarter and there, not fifty feet away, he could see the surf breaking over the edge of the reef. It was now or never. Ringing for full speed, he ordered hard left rudder, hoping to take the ship straight into the teeth of the storm and move her ahead.

But *Adler* did not respond at all. Captain Fritze was so unlucky as to be directly in the path of the current that was sweeping along the western reef; at best his ship could make 11 knots; and in this storm she could not even maintain headway against waves and wind and currents.

Now, very late in the game, Captain Fritze decided to make his attempt to run *Adler* into shore and beach her beside the Americans' *Nipsic.* It would mean slipping the chains of the single bower remaining, turning almost around to starboard, hoping for the extra push of a squall, and something more from the engines to straighten out the ship and run her straight ashore.

Even as Captain Fritze made ready to give the order, the storm changed everything. A particularly vicious wave struck *Adler* on her starboard beam and carried her stern around to touch the reef. She did not seem to touch hard, but when the contact was broken, so was the ship's rudder. She swung back away from the reef but broadside on it, and hung, suspended by her single starboard anchor.

Now Captain Fritze knew he had no chance at all, not even the half of a chance. All he could possibly do was to take desperate action.

He raised his voice and began shouting orders as quickly

as he could spit them out, not that he was panicking, but he had nearly no time at all to do what was necessary for his brave and loyal crew.

"All men on deck!" he shouted. The word was passed. The cooks and bakers came up from below, and the black gang stopped the engines, let off the steam, and came charging up the gangways.

"Man the boats, ready the davits," came the order.

Carefully, precisely, the men went to their positions, manning boats and davits, and the first boat was gotten away, off the starboard—now leeward—side, and the three men who managed to clamber into it made their way to shore and safety.

Captain Fritze had ordered the men into their cork life vests, and most of them hastened to put them on.

He looked over again to port. The *Adler* was approaching the reef too closely. Time had run out, and none—or nearly none—was left. Not another boat could be gotten away.

"Ready to slip the chain," he ordered First Officer Arend, and Arend and his men were there, ready to comply.

The Captain looked to port and to starboard. A huge wave was descending on them, and as it came, he captured its rhythm and made ready to use the sea itself in one last attempt to save his men.

"Slip the chain," he shouted, as the surge of the wave brought up under the *Adler*'s keel. The chain was slipped without letting the wave lose an ounce of its power, and the huge rolling sea took *Adler* by her bottom and shook her, and threw her up on the top of the reef, on her port beam ends. The rattling shock threw nearly every man overboard. Captain Fritze was catapulted against the bridge rail and gashed his head, but managed to hang on aboard ship. There she lay, atop the reef, canted at 90 degrees, but her deck was not only at right angles to the water, it was facing inshore—which meant protection from the sea and storm. Of the crew, some twenty men were washed into the current that raged along the reef and were drowned, but most of the rest managed to clamber back aboard the deck, where they clung to guns and masts. Some managed to swim to land, including *Lieutenant zur See* Souchon, who could never remember how he made it from the reef to the shore in front of the American consulate, but somehow he did manage to save himself. Most of the men scrambled through the shallow water atop the reef and came back aboard, and in their efforts to save themselves were many acts of heroism. First Officer Arend was knocked unconscious and thrown into the water, where the current threatened to wash him to the bottom. He was saved by *Oberhandwerfer* Sohn, who had made the safety of the deck when he saw the stricken officer slipping by him, who did not hesitate for a moment, but plunged into the roaring surf and dragged *Kapitänlieutenant* von Arend to the comparative safety of the wrecked ship's deck. Lieutenant Caesar was being washed away when his clothing was grasped by *Obermatrosen* Meyer, and he was hauled to safety and a new chance for life.

The men of the *Adler* had not come off scot-free. There were a hundred broken bones in the hulk that lay atop the reef, and as to safety, these men were as far away from shore, in this raging storm, as if they had been on another island. They were clinging to a useless hulk, blown and battered by the storm, but they were alive, and there was hope for all but the twenty who had been swept away. It was very little, but it was more than even Captain Fritze had expected.

CHAPTER TWELVE

Day of Death—9 a.m.

As THE 170 officers and men of the *Nipsic* were brought from water's edge to the American consulate, every man was either examined or asked whether he had some complaint for the attention of Surgeon Derr, and the sick and wounded were accommodated in the consulate.

Lieutenant Fillette's Marine guards put aside their rifles and handed out dry shirts and trousers to the sopping sailors. Now two problems remained: to prepare and serve food to the hungry crew members, who had not eaten a meal since noon on Friday, and to organize the men to maintain discipline now that they were so suddenly thrust ashore in unfamiliar surroundings.

The ship's executive officer, Lieutenant Hawley, went back to the beach to watch over the *Nipsic,* and the responsibility for maintaining order was left in the hands of Captain Mullan and Lieutenant R. G. Davenport, the navigating officer. But overcome by the shock and strain through which they had lived, neither officer rose to the occasion to keep the crew together and find occupation for them.

Consul Blacklock had neither the facilities, the time, nor

the experience in command of men to handle the unruly crew of the *Nipsic*. Nor were his relations with Captain Mullan such as to inspire confidence. The Consul was shocked at the behavior of captain and crew, and it showed. Not a single life need have been lost, he said bitterly that day, had Captain Mullan kept his wits about him, and had the officers been in control of the crew of the *Nipsic*. Not one man who remained aboard the vessel was drowned or seriously hurt. The dead were the panicky swimmers and the unfortunate occupants of the gig who were sent out to undertake the impossible and unnecessary task of carrying a line that could have been thrown ashore, and eventually was.

The crew of the *Nipsic* had earned a reputation for lawlessness in other ports, at San Francisco and in Hawaii, which meant, of course, that Captain Mullan was a bad disciplinarian and failed to run a taut ship. On this morning of March 16th the Captain proved the charge beyond question. By nine o'clock all the *Nipsic*'s crew had been cared for, and Surgeon Derr and his pharmacist's mate were able to slow down and devote their skills to the handful of men suffering seriously from injuries or exposure.

The rest of the crew of the *Nipsic* might have been moved to the Evangelical Church, to a nearby warehouse of the MacArthur company, or back to the beach. Had the junior officers been in control, such action would have been taken (as became apparent later), but Captain Mullan was still in command, whether or not he chose to exercise his function, and in the absence of Lieutenant Hawley the junior officers had no one on whom to lean.

By eight o'clock the able men of the crew of *Nipsic* had begun to wander into the town seeking food, drink, and a chance to tell strangers of the harrowing experiences they had undergone and the heroism they had displayed. They wandered aimlessly up and down the streets, or made for

Mr. Moors's hotel and other saloons along the row. A handful got something to eat for themselves, but most of these rough sailors sought greater stimulation, and the storekeepers and bartenders were only too glad to provide free drinks for the unlucky victims of the storm.

Soon the men were feeling the effects of their liquor. Most of them were soaked again, from walking around in the rain and wind, and several groups began moving back toward the consulate, expecting to have dry clothes given them once again. They also wanted money, food, and the chance to send messages immediately to their families.

Of course Consul Blacklock could not supply any of these wants, and some of the men began to grow ugly. In disgust, Blacklock turned the matter over to Lieutenant Fillette and asked him to preserve order at the consulate. A mob began to assemble outside the building, with several leaders telling the men they must demand their "rights." As the crowd grew ugly, Lieutenant Fillette saw that it was time to move, and he stood on the steps of the consulate and warned the sailors of the *Nipsic* that he would not brook any interference with his guard or any attempt to disturb the Consul in his work.

So mattters stood before nine o'clock, ashore.

Aboard the *Trenton* Admiral Kimberly had given up his concern over the source of the storm and was listening with growing worry to the reports of the ship's declining seaworthiness. The barometer was rising, but the wind was now blowing from due north, which meant straight down the gullet of the harbor. This change in the wind was more vital to *Trenton* than to any other ship, because her defective hawsepipes began to ship more water onto the berth deck, and in spite of the hand-bailing to which half the crew was now put, the water was gaining in the engine room. Lieutenant Commander Lyon's men had begun by stuffing jackasses, or hawse bags, into the hawseholes, then shoring up this stuffing with hammocks, using grease and every other possible device to keep the water out. But the hawsepipes were low down on the berth deck, and the *Trenton* was a full-bowed ship, which meant that she plunged deep when she put her nose down. All the steam pumps were going, and so were the hand pumps and so were the buckets, but with the shift of the wind to due north, the sea began gaining on the men.

Lieutenant Commander Lyon took personal charge of the bow, supervising the men as they tried first one way and then another to keep the hawsepipes filled, so the water could not get in.

From time to time Lieutenant Commander Lyon moved up to the gun deck where Gunner Westfall and his volunteers were fighting the battle of the starboard bridle port. Each sea that came smashing against the bow knocked the men flat, but after each sea they would get up and rush back to the barricade to repair it for the attack of the next. They had stopped more than half the water from coming in, but they had not stopped enough. The executive officer sent other men back to get lumber and hammers and nails, and he pulled Westfall aside and told him what must be done to strengthen the barricade. They would shore up the table on both sides with mattresses and stuff the edges with hammocks, and then covering all, they would build a wooden barricade. Also, they would build wooden drainage canals, or flumes, and divert the water into the water closet chutes to keep it from trickling aft, where it would seek the level of the engine room.

Aboard the *Adler,* men with broken heads and broken bones were lying on the port bulkheads of the starboard cabins, for now the port bulkheads had become the ship's deck, such as it was. Surgeon Tereszkiewicz had his hands full; most of his medical equipment was lost or washed overboard, and nearly every man on the ship needed some medical attention. Captain Fritze was suffering from concussion and a bad head cut, but he never lost the power of command or his ability to convince officers and men that somehow he would bring them out of this catastrophe alive. If ever a situation existed in which a ship's crew might be expected to panic, here it was: the *Adler* lay not two hundred yards from the safety of land; her masts had broken off with the shock of the dumping on the reef, and she was no longer a ship but a protective hulk for the crew, but in a way she also seemed to be a death trap, for the men could not escape her.

On shore Seumanu Tafa tried to launch a boat to take a line to the *Adler,* moving under the suspicious eyes of Consul Knappe and his fifty armed sailors and Marines. But no canoe could brave the tempestuous waters; luckily, the canoes were upset almost as they left the shore, and the Samoans swam back before they were caught by the undertow.

The Germans tried to fire a signal gun carrying a light line, and they fired it often. But the wreck of the *Adler* lay at a 45-degree angle from the sandy beach, almost directly across the reef from the old German consulate. A projectile from a life-saving gun was blown immediately back toward the shore, landing no closer than the light west of the mouth of the Mulivai. In this wind the only chance so to reach the *Adler* would have been from the point at Matautu, and the distance was far too great. The surf washed constantly across the *Adler,* over the reef, and made it impossible for the men on board to venture onto her slippery sides. With the change in wind, the seas splashed higher across the hull. For better or for worse, the men of the *Adler* would ride out the storm aboard their vessel.

The proud *Calliope* was also sorely affected by the change in the wind and the rising of the already mountainous seas. The lashings of the foreyard carried away, the yard from the foremast; the spar then swayed about dangerously from side to side as the ship rolled, imperiling the mast until Gunner's Mate William Elgie moved up to the topgallant forecastle and—disregarding the mortal danger to himself—managed to lash the yard to the mast again. As he worked, a piece of flotsam was carried over the bows and smashed him in the face, but he never stopped; bleeding, he finished the job and then staggered back into the arms of his mates.

For the first time, with the changing of the wind, Captain Kane began to have serious fears for the safety of his ship. He ordered all the watertight doors between compartments dogged down. (*Calliope* was of much more modern interior design than any of the American or German vessels.) The anchors were not holding, and the sheet was causing more trouble than it seemed to be worth. Captain Kane ordered the sheet cable slipped, and more steam in the boilers; he would have to rely on steam to do what the anchors should do in decent weather.

Calliope was now sandwiched between *Olga* on her starboard side and *Vandalia* on her port. Oddly enough, while *Vandalia* was on the weather side, *Olga* was charging and plunging the more madly and endangered the British warship the more. In spite of all that Captain von Erhardt could do, *Olga* bore down on *Calliope,* nearly ramming her, and it was only because Captain Kane sheered off with rudder and full speed that the German ship did not cut the British man-of-war amidships, giving such a blow with her cutwater that even the armored iron and wooden vessel would never have survived. As it was, *Olga*'s bowsprit rammed the loosened foreyard and sprang it badly, carrying away Gunner's Mate

Elgie's new lashings. That was small price for Captain Kane to pay; he saw that the collision between bowsprit and spar had fended *Olga* off and saved his ship.

During the sudden sheer, the strain on the port cable had become more than metal could bear, and the chain parted, leaving the *Calliope* hanging by a single anchor, her starboard bower.

Hardly had *Calliope* sheered away from *Olga* than she was struck by a gargantuan sea that stove in three more boats, and then as the spray cleared, Captain Kane could see that *Vandalia* was drifting down on him. He was steering ahead, steaming at 60 revolutions to clear the reef, which was close under *Calliope*'s stern. He could not stop or back. So *Calliope* put her jib boom into *Vandalia*'s starboard quarter gallery and carried it away. Then the two ships were apart again. Just after 8:45 *Vandalia,* carried by a sudden shift in the wind, moved back to her old position.

But not for long. Less than fifteen minutes later *Vandalia* was again stern to *Calliope*'s bow and dropping down fast. *Calliope* was in a dreadful predicament, with her stern only a few feet from the reefs; Captain Kane came up close under the stern of *Vandalia* and attempted to sheer off to starboard, but before the ship would answer her helm, her bowsprit was over *Vandalia*'s stern, carrying away the fastenings, and losing her jib boom, dolphin striker, and both whisker gaffs. The bowsprit was saved only because the ship stood nearly on end as her bow went down, and then the jib fell back into place as the ship rose again. *Vandalia* was saved from ramming by the prow of *Calliope* only because at the last minute Captain Kane decided to save her.

"Ease the engines," he told the navigator, Lieutenant Pearson, just before the crash. "We won't run him down. Give him another chance."

So the *Calliope*'s engines were stopped, and for a moment they were put astern, to try to avoid the disaster that threatened the American ship at that moment.

Captain Kane saved the *Vandalia* with his gallant gesture, but he placed his own ship in mortal danger. Before he reversed engines, *Calliope*'s rudder was ten feet from the lip of the reef; after that maneuver the distance was cut to a fathom.

Caught between *Olga, Vandalia,* and the reef, Captain Kane had no more margin for maneuver. He could not do what he so admired Captain Fritze for doing; *Calliope* was a ship of 2,800 tons, three and a half times the size of *Adler;* the big British ship would not be lifted up and cast high and dry on the reef; she would smash against the coral, the rocky knives would eat through her side, and she would be sucked under as had been the little *Eber.*

What was to be done?

Captain Kane had only one course. He could try to go outside. *Calliope,* with her tandem athwartship engines and six cylindrical boilers, was capable of 3000 horsepower. Her cruising speed was 10 knots, but at full power she could make 13¾ knots, and under forced draft she could add at least a knot to that speed. Of course it would be forced draft, and more—everything Staff Engineer H. G. Bourke could give him. Even so, the course was studded with "ifs" making it as dangerous as an uncharted passage. They would make it *if* the engines would stand the strain, *if* these engines could generate the power to drive the ship against wind and sea—and who knew at this moment how much power that would take? They would be safe *if* the ship would answer her helm, and Captain Kane was under no illusions that it was certain she would answer; he had ten men at that wheel, but they faced a storm the like of which he had never seen.

(Not long before, the storm had carried away *Trenton's* wheel—smashing every spoke in it.)

The *Calliope* might be saved *if* Captain Kane got enough intervals of clear weather so that he could see reef and harbor entrance, and *if* wheel, rudder, and relieving tackles would stand the strain that would be put upon them, strain far greater than anything envisaged by the designers or constructors at Portsmouth Dockyard.

If everything went well, and if every part of the ship surpassed its expectations, only then might *Calliope* be saved. It was fortunate that *Calliope* was the ship she was, or there would have been no hope. She was the tenth ship of the *Comus* class to be launched, a group of unarmored cruisers that could dispense with docking because they boasted coppered bottoms. Being tenth of her class, *Calliope* was considerably improved over the prototype; she had greater displacement and greater engine power; her breadth (44 feet 6 inches) was the same as that of the other ships of her class, but her length (235 feet) was ten feet more than that of any of the others. True, her depth of hold was greater, and she drew more water than her sister ships, but while her weight was 390 tons more than that of the others, her horsepower was 600 horses greater, and although the specifications stated her speed at $13\frac{3}{4}$ knots, she had a reserve power greater than any other ship of her class. Call it fortune or fate that had brought her to Samoa instead of *Comus* or *Canada,* for example; at least she had the better chance.

As Captain Kane reasoned so quickly—every second counting—he allowed himself one small margin, if it could even be called that. The ship might respond and try, but fail to make way against the storm. Then the Captain would put the helm to starboard and try to beach her on the sand at the base of Point Matautu where there was a landing for small boats, south of the innermost point of the outer eastern reef. This unprotected beach was no place for the ship, the Captain thought, but at least here he might save the crew, if not the *Calliope*. The first danger was the Shore Reef, a fathom from his rudder; the second was the outer reef, which he might strike without ever seeing it in the ferocious squalls that swept across his bridge. But there was really no choice, unless he wished to stand for another few seconds and watch his ship spit herself on the ugly coral behind him. Already he had eighteen inches of water in his wardroom.

Just before 9:30, the Captain made up his mind and sent a messenger below to Staff Engineer Bourke, telling what he intended to do and asking for every pound of steam the engineering department could give him.

Engineer Bourke heard, and made ready to do what was necessary at the signal from the telegraph. His men heard, and the word was passed around the room and in to the stokers. Not a sound came from the men, except the noises of firing up. Not a man asked a question or gave a sign of fear.

The Staff Engineer made ready to give the ship all the forced draft she would take and blessed the Westport coal and the competence of his maintenance men. If ever a ship was ready for such a trial, he was confident that *Calliope* was her name.

The bells tinkled from above, calling for full speed, and Engineer Bourke moved swiftly to the boilers himself.

On deck Captain Kane ordered the cable of the starboard bower slipped; *Calliope* shuddered and headed into the teeth of the storm; the green seas flooded over her bows with force enough to sink a ship as small as *Adler*. Captain Kane sheered well out to starboard of *Vandalia*; the ship stood perfectly still, neither losing nor gaining an inch, her engines roaring and her screw racing in the water. Then, suddenly, she began to move, pitching with tremendous lurches, first bow under water, then stern—but when the stern was under, the propeller had its effect. One could not say *Calliope* was making half a knot, even, but she was moving—it could be counted in feet—one, two, three—and every second brought her another few inches away from the lip of the reef.

CHAPTER THIRTEEN

Day of Death—10 a.m.

F ROM THE point of view of Captain Kane of the *Calliope,*
the German *Olga* and the American *Vandalia* had been
charging recklessly about the harbor, but from the vantage
point of the *Vandalia* it was *Calliope* that was "running
amuck," as one of *Vandalia*'s officers put it.

The fact was that after midnight of March 15th, not a
single vessel in Apia harbor was completely under the control
of its officers, and as the storm moved to its midday height,
the ships were less and less controllable.

When *Calliope* struck *Vandalia* for the second time just
before nine o'clock in the morning, the damage was relatively
light and did not worry Lieutenant Carlin nearly so much
as an occurrence a few minutes earlier, when the steering
gear had carried away. One reason *Vandalia* seemed to Captain Kane on *Calliope* to handle so sloppily was that she was
being steered by her relieving tackles.

The loss of the starboard quarter gallery was of little
importance to the overall safety of the ship—but another
result of the collision was far more doleful. When *Calliope*'s
bowsprit struck, the water gauge glass in one of *Vandalia*'s

boilers broke, and steam and water began pouring out into the engine room under a pressure of 60 pounds.

The scene created in the engine room, then, was that of some special hell for sailors. The violent pitching of the ship lifted the screw out of the water, and the engines, relieved of all load but their own friction, increased to a terrifying velocity, nearly deafening the engine-room crew. Then the stern settled into a wave, just as the bow pointed to the sky, and the instantaneous increase of load on the propeller caused the engines to stop dead *for ten seconds,* the longest ten seconds in Engineer Harrie Webster's life. The engines labored, then began driving the propeller again; for a moment the sound was normal, then the propeller was out of water, and the screaming and the cacophony began again.

It was bad enough before, with the hot pipes and over-heated engines hissing off steam as the cold seawater poured down into the engine room; when the glass broke, the steam was increased a dozen-fold, the men were blinded, and the whole vast cavern was filled with hissing and white cloud.

The steam in the affected boiler had to be shut off, but this was more of an undertaking than it might seem. The deck was rolling in water, and the ship was pitching and tossing so badly that no man could walk to the boilers to turn the valve and shut off the steam. Engineer Webster did not even try—he ordered the fires hauled from the boiler and ordered it disconnected from the remainder of the battery. In that way, the boiler could be put out of action without endangering the life of any man.

It was easier said than done.

The straining of the ship had caused the valve to this boiler to stick, and although the fire was hauled, the boiler could not be disconnected from the others. Instead of adding to the ship's power, the broken boiler was taking it away, acting as a sort of condenser to draw off steam from the other working boilers.

The ship was demanding 42 revolutions to steam ahead to relieve her anchors, but the steam gauges began to drop in all boilers.

60 pounds
57 pounds
52 pounds
48 pounds

Two minutes had gone by, and Webster and his men were struggling with the stuck valve that would disengage the faulty boiler.

42 pounds
37 pounds
32 pounds

The revolutions had dropped from 42 to 26.

Engineer Webster was so busy below, struggling with the stuck valve, that he could only hear the importuning cast down the engine-room hatch—he could not take his eyes from his work long enough to look up.

"For God's sake, Webster," came an anguished voice, "give her more steam. We're lost, we're lost."

The valve still stuck, and the wrench slipped in Engineer Webster's sweaty hand.

30 pounds
28 pounds
27 pounds

"Open her out!" came the cry from above. "We're on the reef. Go faster, go faster!"

At last, as the needles in the gauges quivered at 27 pounds, the stuck valve yielded, the hissing of steam from the broken gauge trailed away and stopped, and the needles in the gauges began rising jerkily.

In the engine room the sound of the screw picked up in

intensity. The revolutions marched up from 18 to 20, to 22, to 28, to 32, to 42, and then the *Vandalia* seemed secure again, and there was no more terrified crying down the engine-room hatch. In a few minutes Executive Officer Carlin came to the hatch and asked Webster how it was going. Webster was able to grin and give him a positive report.

"No water in the bilge. Everything working well."

A few minutes later, a pale Captain Schoonmaker appeared at the open hatch to ask how long Webster could keep his engines running to give them at least 42 revolutions.

"All day long," said Engineer Webster.

The Captain looked relieved and withdrew without another word.

While Webster was talking, his men were repairing the broken steam gauge, and in fifteen minutes they had it back together, sound as before, and the fires were relighted in the boiler. Never again, as long as the ship floated, would the engineering department give the ship less than 60 pounds pressure.

Shortly after nine o'clock, when this crisis had been surmounted, Engineer Webster left his post for a few minutes and made his way through spray and water to Surgeon Harvey's dispensary. He returned bearing enough whisky to give every man in the fire room a two-ounce drink.

The men needed the stimulant. Since midnight, when the call for all hands had come, no one in the engineering department had been away from duty for more than a moment, and they had not tasted food or drink. The galley was awash, the decks were afloat, and the sea pouring down the hatches had found its way into the ship's water tanks and spoiled the drinking water. Hot as they were, exhausted and weak from thirst, not a man belowdecks had quit, although two of the water tenders showed such definite signs of giving out that Webster ordered them to take it easy. As for the others, from

Machinist Gibson to the lowest coal-heaver, they stood at their posts and acknowledged orders with a will. There was no lack of morale in *Vandalia*'s engine room, even though, far more than the men above, those below could tell that the ship's anchors were dragging. The drag came with an occasional strange jerking motion of the ship that told the engine-room crew that the anchors were moving closer together.

At 9:30 Engineer Webster was on his high perch when a seaman stopped long enough at the hatch to shout down that *Calliope* was putting out to sea. Webster relayed the news to the crew, and it gave them all a lift, for it meant one of their hazards was eliminated, and it showed the men that ships could steam ahead through this storm.

With his men weakening, Engineer Webster asked for help from the deck, and Sergeant Coleman of the Marine guard and several of his men came down as volunteer firemen and coal-heavers, to give the regulars a rest.

By ten o'clock, Engineer Webster had the definite feeling that the ship was dragging onto the reef and that it would not be much longer before they struck. The strange, jerking motions came more frequently, and he could tell by the amount of water the hatch was taking that the seas were breaking over the ship either broadside or nearly beam-on.

On deck, Lieutenant Carlin could feel the end coming, too. For an hour the ship had veered, reaching out fifty feet from the reef at its farthest swing on the anchors, lolling back to within twenty feet of the coral that stuck out like a table top above the cavern below. He allowed himself to consider, for a moment, whether they would be tossed up, like the *Adler,* or thrown down under the reef edge, like the *Eber* and the *Peter Godeffroy.* Each time the *Vandalia* swung back toward the reef, she came a little bit nearer its teeth.

Although the wind was howling, Lieutenant Carlin had

ordered the rigging of a spanker on the mizzenmast, but as the ship swept in close to the Shore Reef and its inshore current, he found that spanker, helm, and two anchors on the weather bow were not enough to keep *Vandalia*'s head into the wind, and the more the anchors dragged, the more the ship was sucked into the current, and the more Engineer Webster noticed the seas coming in beam-on.

Captain Schoonmaker had recovered, to an extent, from his weakening injuries of the long night of horror, and he was on the poop, in overall command of his ship. Carlin was a good lieutenant; he deferred to his Captain's judgment when deference was in order, and he was capable, as he had shown, of taking command in an emergency and relinquishing it with grace when the crisis ended.

Lieutenant Carlin pointed out the deficiences of the ship and their position, and the problems they faced. At 2,100 tons, *Vandalia* was only rated as a 12-knot ship, and if she was unable to breast the current next to the reef, how could she steam out? They looked outward to *Calliope,* which had been steaming steadily for nearly an hour and had not yet reached a point opposite *Trenton,* halfway out to the entrance to the harbor, and the far edge of the reef. There was their answer: *Calliope* was a much bigger and stronger ship, and she was barely making it, if she made it at all. The Captain and his executive officer knew that *Vandalia* did not have a chance of steaming out of the harbor.

The only possible solution was to take advantage of the current that ran along the reef, go with it, and beach the *Vandalia* next to *Nipsic* on the sand. There was a narrow space off *Nipsic*'s port side, between the mouth of the Vaisingano and the end of the reef, and if they could reach this place, the ship ought to be in close enough for rescue of the crew.

At 10:30 Captain Schoonmaker gave his assent, and Lieutenant Carlin ordered the men in the bow to make ready to slip the bower chains. The sheet chain was slipped first, to avoid fouling the ground tackle of *Olga*, which was riding inshore of *Vandalia*, perhaps twenty feet off the reef at her closest point of pitch and yaw.

The Lieutenant gave the order and telegraphed for full speed ahead at the same time. Using the anchors for the last time, *Vandalia* veered inshore to the reef to pass behind *Olga*, then slipped her bower chains and did pass, with ten feet to spare on either side, between the German man-of-war and the reef.

After passing the *Olga*, Captain Schoonmaker made a determined effort to head back to port, to take the ship's head into the wind, but it was as he and Lieutenant Carlin had known—the *Vandalia* simply did not respond; the current and the storm were too much for her. So they turned the ship's bow to shore, and aimed for the soft spot to the starboard side of *Nipsic*.

Captain Schoonmaker nearly made his landfall. He would have made it, had not the rushing current of the Vaisingano interfered with him. But the bow of *Vandalia* was caught in the outrushing current of the river, while the stern was borne along by the inrushing current caused by the suction of the undercut reef. Ten feet more and the ship would have been safe, but the ten feet were missing. The *Vandalia* came on until her bow struck in the soft sand a hundred yards from shore, forty yards off the stem of *Nipsic*. The current of the Vaisingano pushed her bow and the current along the reef pulled her stern until the ship lay broadside to the wind, and the *Vandalia* took the point of the reef with her stern. It was 10:45.

CHAPTER FOURTEEN

Day of Death—11 a.m.

As it seemed on deck, the *Vandalia* struck easily enough and swung around gently to present her port side to the weather, but down below, the crash of her striking sent every man sprawling, and then the ship began such a creaking and groaning that it seemed every timber was protesting the fate she knew nature had in store for her.

Captain Schoonmaker was in the cabin with a number of other officers, and the remainder of the deck officers were on the poop or under it. Most of the men were still seeking shelter under the forecastle, although a few were on the gun deck. On the poop, Lieutenant Carlin kept the engines going until he was certain that *Vandalia* was hard aground, and then he ordered them stopped.

Hardly had that order been flung down the engine-room hatch when came another.

"Abandon ship!"

At such an order the engine room of the *Nipsic* had panicked, and the men had nudged and pushed one another aside in their haste to speed up the ladders and escape the undersea trap. No such disgraceful conduct accompanied the abandonment of *Vandalia*'s engine room. Everything was done exactly as it would have been done had the ship been coming in to anchor on the finest day of the year.

Engineer Webster walked into the fire room to give the order to the stokers, and they began evacuating the room quietly, without apparent fear.

The shock of the grounding had caused most of the steam gauges to break, and the fire room quickly filled with steam, so that Engineer Webster took some time in making sure that every man had gone above. Then he moved into the engine room to make a similar check, and before he started up himself, he paused for a moment to open one of the main safety valves, to prevent a possible explosion.

By the time Engineer Webster was ready to leave the engine room, water had begun pouring over the weather side of *Vandalia*. The ship had swung full broadside to the sea, and had begun to fill through the hole in her stern. The weather rail was soon awash, and the combers came dashing completely over the ship. The storm was approaching its peak as *Vandalia* struck, and the wind was blowing from due north and making ready to shift to the west, which at this particular time was the most disadvantageous point from which it could blow on *Vandalia*.

The ship was within two hundred yards of dry land and safety, but within minutes seas were breaking fifteen feet above the port rail, and the water about *Vandalia* on the lee side was a maelstrom, slashed by the Vaisingano current going out and the reef current coming in.

Literally, the sea boiled, and looking down from the poop Lieutenant Carlin could tell that it would be reckless to try to swim ashore.

Inshore the beach was strewn with wreckage of every type: ladders, spars, hammocks, broken oars and broken boat timbers, casks, gratings, pots and pans, deck lamps, and pieces of chain. Already bodies were beginning to wash up, the twisted bodies of German sailors from the *Eber* and the *Adler* and Americans from the *Nipsic*.

Soon the skylights of the cabin were washed off, and the seas began pouring in, forcing the Captain and the other officers to join Lieutenant Carlin on the poop. Water surged across the main deck and into the forecastle, and the men began climbing for the rigging.

Engineer Webster was ready to come up from the engine room less than fifteen minutes after the ship struck. He paused for a moment, wondering if he might not take time to go to his cabin and save a few of his belongings. But his mind was changed quickly when he found a fireman named Melville wandering back in the engine room. Melville said it was impossible to reach the deck by way of the after hatch. The water was pouring over the stern and the port side in such volume that a man would be thrown back down and killed, perhaps, or knocked unconscious and drowned.

Engineer Webster and Fireman Melville reversed direction and snaked their way along the catwalk to the berth deck, then stumbled forward holding each other, aiming for the dim light they could see ahead—light that represented the forehatch.

As they moved forward, these two men were punched to the deck time after time by the bumping of the ship on the bottom as the seas smashed her. The closer they came to the hatch, the worse their situation became, because the pipe that supplied steam to the capstan engine under the top-gallant forecastle had burst, and the berth deck was so fogged they could scarcely see ahead of them. Engineer Webster was now acutely aware of danger. Through the mist he saw Ensign Heath bound on some mission; he stopped the Ensign and called his attention to the fact that every man was out of the engine room; he wanted that known in case Heath should survive and he should not. The Ensign was too busy to listen, and he brushed Engineer Webster aside.

Webster and Fireman Melville struggled on. They reached the hatch, which was immediately abaft the break of the forecastle, and scrambled on deck near the galley. They rushed under the forecastle to seize lashed hammocks as life preservers, and for a moment they remained under the starboard side of the forecastle, for that seemed to be a safe place. Water was pouring over the topgallant forecastle, but the spar deck had only two feet of water in it; the port forward pivot port was still secure even in this sea.

Soon, however, the place of safety became a place of immediate peril. The port bridle ports were stove in by the smashing waves. The port pivot port was carried away, and suddenly, the men huddled here found themselves up to their necks in water. They began scrambling for the ladders that would lead them to the topgallant forecastle.

Engineer Webster threw aside the hammock, which was only weighing him down, and made a dash for the starboard ladder. The waves were now breaking inside the ship, and the water was five feet deep. He lost his footing, was cast headlong into the water, and began grasping for the side of the ship to find ropes or a rail on which to fix his fingers. So hard did he clutch that all his fingernails, softened by many hours in the water, were turned back.

Earlier in the morning, Engineer Webster had removed his socks and loosened his shoelaces so that he could kick off his shoes at any time that he might have to swim for life. He kicked them off now, and floundered in the water until his hand grasped a rope that was made fast at its upper end to something above. Climbing and sprawling, he made his way to the topgallant forecastle and collapsed, shaking in exhaustion.

From the forecastle, Harrie Webster gained an idea of the

condition of the ship and the danger the crew now faced. The sea was breaking into the ship with ease, water was pouring through all the hatches, and *Vandalia* was settling; he could tell she was filling because debris came floating up through the forehatch. He saw a wooden chair float by, cocked at a crazy angle. Up came mattresses, hammocks, pieces of lumber, and a sailor's blouse. The wreckage came floating up out of the ship, washed across the bulwarks, and covered the sea inshore with flotsam. Engineer Webster noted idly that it was dangerous to swimmers for all that wreckage to be out there. Not that he had any idea of trying to swim ashore; one look at the madly churning sea beneath the *Vandalia*'s starboard was enough, and had it not been enough, Webster watched as a sailor flung himself into the sea and tried to swim the two hundred yards to safety. The man went underwater and then came up, took two strokes toward shore, then was caught in the maelstrom and sucked under. He did not appear again.

Within an hour after the *Vandalia* struck, the seas were washing so high over the decks that they endangered the officers on the poop and the men on the forecastle. Captain Schoonmaker was standing on the poop, surrounded by Paymaster Arms, Pay Clerk Roche, and Lieutenant Sutton. Lieutenant Carlin was by the Captain's side, supporting him whenever a wave struck and lapped over them. Two or three times the Captain lost his footing in the water and was washed nearly to the rail, only to be rescued.

But in fifteen minutes Lieutenant Carlin was reduced to holding the Captain with one hand and the rail with the other.

As the seas increased their fierce attack on the ship, it became apparent to Lieutenant Carlin that he must go into the rigging, and so must the Captain, if they were to survive. Carlin spoke to the Captain, who nodded, but was too weak to make the climb. Captain Schoonmaker clung to the rail, and Carlin clung to him for dear life; Carlin insisted again, but the Captain said he was not strong enough to climb into the rigging.

Several of the officers who had been able to grasp life preservers offered these to the Captain, but he waved them away.

Carlin grew desperate. Watching the sea, he waited until a wave swept over them, then leaped into the rigging himself and reached down a hand to the Captain to draw him up. Just then a huge wave struck *Vandalia* on her port quarter and submerged the poop deck entirely, so strong a surge from the sea that a machine gun standing on the deck was washed from its fastenings and smashed overboard. As Lieutenant Carlin reached out his hand, the wave struck Captain Schoonmaker and washed him overboard, too; the Captain sank without a cry or a struggle.

The same wave washed over Lieutenant Sutton. The Lieutenant had spent the night on deck fighting the sea, and he was already exhausted. He did not struggle, either, against the wave that took him.

Paymaster Arms and Pay Clerk Roche were lying on the deck, virtually exhausted from the last half-hour of pounding, holding onto the bottom of the rail. When the sea struck, Paymaster Arms sank in a moment and drowned. His body came to the surface in a few minutes and washed around the bow of the *Vandalia* for half an hour.

Pay Clerk Roche was swept over the stem to the *Nipsic,* some forty yards away, and was able to grasp a rope that hung down there. He was a heavy, fleshy man, however, and was so nearly exhausted that he could not pull himself up onto the deck of the ship. He held the rope for a time, but his hold was broken, and he was swept along the starboard side of the *Nipsic* in full view of his companions, head up, hands clutching. He grasped another rope that trailed from

Nipsic's stern, but he was too weak to hold it, and the sea swept him under; his head came up briefly, and he sank.

From the shore, it became apparent very quickly after the *Vandalia* struck that her officers and men were in mortal danger, even though the ship was close on to the beach. Less than half an hour after striking, the watchers could observe the settling of the ship as she filled with water and wondered if anyone could live in the seas that broke above her decks by twenty feet and more.

By 11:30, from the shore it seemed that every space on the ratlines and the yards was occupied by human beings, and men were climbing into the tops.

After the deaths of the four officers who were swept off the poop, the other officers of *Vandalia* all leaped for the rigging, and as the decks sank, they were deserted.

What a sad and desolate sight the *Vandalia* made, her men clinging like flies to the rigging, most of them nearly naked, their clothing either discarded or blown off their backs as they clustered on the ropes and spars, victims of the merciless fury of wind and wave.

At 11:30 a party of Americans on the shore tried to bring help to the men of *Vandalia*. Consul Blacklock and three officers of the *Nipsic* secured a hawser from that stranded ship and attached a light line to the heavy ropes. Lieutenant Shearman, Ensign Purcell, and Ensign Jones then went scouting on the beach until they found three Samoans who volunteered to swim into the surf with the line. There was some talk about taking a boat, but Chief Seumanu Tafa said no boat could live for a minute in the storm, and that idea was abandoned.

The three Samoans moved to a spot on the beach west of the *Vandalia*, across the reef from the ship. They waded into the water as far as they could go, then stopped, tied the line to their bodies, and began to swim for the *Vandalia*, hoping that the current would carry them down onto the ship. From the shore came shouts of encouragement as the watchers saw the swimmers coming near, so near it seemed that their scheme could not fail. But as the men struck out into the full force of the current, surging seas caught them and swept them down past the *Vandalia*. Expert swimmers that they were, they were like fish in a cataract. They came near, only a few yards from the ship, yet they might have been a thousand yards away for all the good they did; then they were debouched upon the beach, tumbled over and over, and flung onto the sand, gasping for breath.

As the three Samoans lay panting just above the line of the surf, Seumanu Tafa came up and urged others to try. More swimmers went out, and were thrown back on the beach. The line became fouled in the wreckage that seemed to float everywhere in the water. One time the line caught around a broken spar and dragged under the wharf in front of the Naval Hospital; Ensign Jones jumped into the water to free the line, but just as he did so, he was struck from behind by a huge wave that sent him pell-mell under the wharf and into the pilings there; a sailor plunged after Jones and rescued him as he lay nearly unconscious in the water.

Soon it became apparent to Seumanu Tafa and all the others that the storm was raging too fiercely to allow the passage of a line by hand, and no gun of sufficient strength could be found on land to do the job, so the watchers on shore must simply stand and wait. The men of *Vandalia* must hold out and save themselves.

Shortly before noon, the Samoans turned to *Adler* in the hope that they would have more success in reaching that vessel with a line. A number of brown-skinned swimmers moved around the shore to a point in front of the old German consulate, which was almost opposite the place where *Adler* lay uneasily on the reef. From shore the rescuers could see the ship stirring as the waves smashed against her keel. From this angle, they could also see the deck and note the presence of men hanging onto stanchions and the spars.

From the shore to the *Adler* any trip that was made must go entirely across the shallows atop the reef, and this trip was difficult and dangerous, but it was *possible,* whereas the trip to *Vandalia* was not.

The men of the *Adler* had been resting uneasily in their topsy-turvy perches for several hours since their ship had gone ashore. Few of them managed to move about the ship in the morning hours; the rain pelted them too hard, and the squalls and seas made visibility dim and footing on the canted ship too treacherous to venture.

During the morning, several attempts had been made to swim a line ashore across the reef, but they had failed. One swimmer finished the trip successfully, carrying a light line. Then a boatload of Samoans tried to follow the line back to the ship, but the storm threw the full weight of their boat against the light line and it broke, leaving the Samoans stranded and barely able to achieve the shore without capsizing. A Samoan swimmer went out to the ship carrying a line, and made the passage safely, but that line broke when an attempt was made to fix a heavy hawser to it. Finally, just before noon, one of the *Adler*'s quartermasters swam ashore carrying a manila line.

This line was affixed to a hawser, and the hawser was dragged across the water above the reef to the ship. Soon men were pulling themselves across the shallows on this hawser, and fifteen sailors of the *Adler* were able to make the trip before the hawser was caught on the sharp coral and broke.

But it had been proved that the rescue of the sailors of the *Adler* was possible, and the attempts never ceased. Another line was taken to shore, and Consul Knappe, who was directing the operations on the beach, found another hawser to bring out. The men who were not too badly hurt to travel thus were soon taken off the ship, and by noon fewer than fifty of the ship's company remained on the hulk. Captain Fritze and every one of his officers remained aboard. He insisted that the men be rescued first, and no officer was to leave the ship until the last injured man had gone. As for the men, those left aboard were the ones who could not trust themselves to the dangerous passage by hawser; they would have to wait until the storm slackened enough so that boats could be brought across the reef to save them.

CHAPTER FIFTEEN

Day of Death—Noon

O N THE *Trenton,* Executive Officer Lyon and his damage
control parties struggled gamely against the water that
poured over their flagship, but by 9:30 in the morning even
the most determined optimist knew that they were fighting
a losing battle. The hawseholes were the worst of it: no
matter what steps were taken, no matter how many plans
Lieutenant Commander Lyon came up with, the water continued to stream into those openings and down through the
berth deck into the engine room.

Before 9:30 Gunner Westfall and his men had completed
their lumber barricade and were flushing the sea out of the
water closet chutes, so very little water was going aft, where
it would trickle down to the engine room. Gunner Westfall
stood back for a moment to admire his handiwork with some
satisfaction.

But only for a moment.

A man came running to the gun deck bearing a message
from the executive officer. The ventilator holes on the spar
deck were open, said the messenger, and the water was pouring in.

Westfall looked around him, and his eye fell on Boatswain's Mate Gray. He asked Gray if he would make the trip up to the forecastle to nail canvas over the holes, and Gray said he would go along. In a few minutes Westfall and Gray moved aft on the gun deck, then up the ladder to the spar deck. When they came to the upper deck, where the water was running free and the waves were splashing over them constantly, they dropped to all fours, crawled through the water to the forecastle, and set to work.

They had not finished the job—they had scarcely begun— when a powerful sea swept across the forecastle. The wave picked up both men as though they had been jackstraws and swept them a hundred feet back on the deck. Gray was carried back for five seconds, then left near the mainmast. Westfall was plunged into a mass of wrecked boats and smashed equipment almost at the foot of the mast, and lost consciousness. When he recovered his senses a few minutes later, two men were dragging him from beneath the wreckage. He tried to stand up, but could not; he had injured his right foot, and he was waterlogged from seawater he had swallowed.

Gunner Westfall was out of action.

Trenton was in nearly the same condition. By ten o'clock, so much water had poured into the hawsepipes and the other openings on deck that the firemen were working in water up to their waists and water was lapping at the bottoms of the fire boxes. The leakage could not be stopped; one by one the boxes filled, and the fires went out, leaving *Trenton* at the mercy of the storm, now no mechanical steamship, but a sailing ship that had lost her rudder and was trying to save herself by riding to her anchors. All that Admiral Kimberly and Captain Farquhar had to work with were the storm trysails, with which they attempted to keep the ship headed into the wind.

As long as *Trenton* had steam, she could use her steam pumps to keep the water down, but the moment the fires failed, the water began gaining. Every able-bodied man was ordered to the pumps, and like a crew of old-time sailormen they worked the brakes, singing the old chanty "Knock a Man Down." There were two hundred men on those pumps, four hundred arms, working in relays against the dreadful power of the sea, with the certain knowledge that they were fighting a losing battle: the hawsepipes alone let in water faster than the pumpers and bailers could expel it.

At noon the barometer aboard *Trenton* rose to 29.29, but within the hour it had fallen to the lowest point of all the storm, to 29.19, and the winds of hurricane force continued to blow without any sign of letup.

The mizzen trysail was the first one set, by brave able-bodied seamen who climbed the mast in this frightful gale. Then others poured oil overboard on the weather side, in an attempt to quiet the anger of the sea. There was little else to be done, except to watch the slack in the chains and pray; Lieutenant B. M. G. Brown, the *Trenton*'s navigating officer, stood on the poop with Admiral Kimberly and Captain Farquhar, and together they watched the inevitable drift of flagship toward reef.

It was nearly noon when *Calliope* came close enough to *Trenton* for Captain Kane to see her condition. *Trenton* was lying low in the water and taking a heavy beating from the sea. From *Calliope*'s point of view, *Trenton* was a hazard that must be passed. The American ship's anchors seemed to be holding well, but that was all that could be said for her. Captain Kane noticed that the *Trenton*'s rudder was broken and slack and the screw was not turning. As Captain Kane watched, Admiral Kimberly ordered the signal "Fires extinguished," which gave the British Captain an indication of the condition inside *Trenton*.

There was only one way for Captain Kane to take the *Calliope* if he hoped to escape the harbor and the reef: he must go between *Trenton* and the sharp pinnacle known as Cape Horn. The seas were tumbling and breaking so far out that it was difficult for the British Captain to estimate distance, but it was certain that he had none too much room for his maneuvering. He headed for the reef, all six boilers building steam, his engines hot and racing, then sheered past the *Trenton*'s stern, coming so close that *Calliope*'s battered foreyard overhung *Trenton*'s quarter as they passed. The *Calliope* cleared the American ship and cleared the reef and then stood out to sea.

As *Calliope* came inching past, the officers and crew of *Trenton* saw her clearly. What a difference between the British ship, smoke churning from her stack, moving under steam away from the danger of the reef, and the helpless American vessel, power gone, sluggish with the weight of seawater in her bowels, fighting a fight that could not be won!

Yet as *Calliope* passed, the officers and men of *Trenton* saw and began to cheer her. The astounded British seamen wondered that the men of the *Trenton* found time to worry about anything other than their own fate—and they responded with a cheer as loud as that of *Trenton*. Then *Calliope* passed on. Five minutes after rounding the stern of *Trenton*, she could no longer be seen, and *Calliope*'s lookouts were scanning east and west, watching anxiously for the reef on both sides. By noon, driving the ship to its utmost, Captain Kane estimated that he was making about a knot against the storm. Soon he felt that the ship had passed outside the reef and was in the open sea; the wind blew harder than ever, but the waves, now unconfined, rolled on toward shore, and the peaks and valleys became less pronounced. Captain Kane reduced his speed from 70 revolutions to 60, and the draft to natural, and steamed out to sea.

The heroism and good fellowship shown on *Calliope* and *Trenton* were in sharp contrast to the actions of the crew of the *Nipsic,* at noon on March 16th the only ship's crew safe ashore in Apia. All morning the men had been congregating around the consulate, making demands, and returning to the saloons for frequent infusions of Dutch courage. Before noon the Marines had been forced into action against the sailors, and several *Nipsic* men sported bruises about the head. Two men were clapped into irons when they became uncontrollable.

After *Vandalia* struck, Lieutenant Shearman and the other officers came back to the consulate to enlist help from the men of the *Nipsic*—and the men *refused to go.* In spite of requests, orders, and pleas, these mutinous seamen would not return to the beach to help their comrades, but wandered about the town, fighting and carousing and keeping the Marines busy trying to control them.

By noon, aboard *Vandalia* the position of the officers and men had grown much worse than it had been an hour earlier. Engineer Webster had been safe enough on the topgallant forecastle, but by noon he had to seek a higher perch, or perish. He climbed to the fife rail of the foremast and secured himself as best he could on the lee side, arms wrapped around the mast, holding on for dear life. Then he found a perch and stood, barefooted, on the coils of rope cast over the pins of the fife rail, one bare arm thrust through the starboard Jacob's ladder, the other hand grasping the running rigging that led aloft. Half a dozen of his men stood with him, standing by the wreck, although mountainous seas swept completely over them every few minutes. Higher up in the starboard fore rigging crouched Assistant Surgeon Cordeiro and Lieutenant Culver, while farther aloft was Surgeon Harvey, who was naked from the waist up because the wind had torn away his shirt before noon. Some men in the ratlines took off their shirts and wrapped them around their feet to relieve the pain of standing; soon most of the crew was half-naked, and some men were totally without clothing.

Engineer Webster and his men had scarcely achieved their tenuous perches when the *Vandalia* began to heel slowly toward the sea. It seemed certain that she was going over—to capsize and dash them all into a crushing surf against the side of their own ship. *Vandalia* heeled until it seemed she could heel no more without slipping over; then the sea caught her and she began to move the other way, but as she moved, the water in her bottom leveled her, deep as it was, and she settled on the sand and did not stir again.

The seas washed higher, and occasionally a man was swept away. Usually the man went overboard and was whisked out to sea, his comrades scarcely able to trace his going from the moment he struck the water. Some were luckier, among them Chief Engineer Greene.

The Chief Engineer had been on the poop with the Captain, and he had been washed overboard three times. Each time he had been able to grasp a rope and pull himself back aboard the ship after the washing sea had passed. Finally, he was overboard and carried so far from the side of the ship that he could not get back, but Chief Engineer Greene was wearing a life preserver and was able to swim the two hundred and fifty yards to the side of the *Nipsic*, where he seized an overhanging rope. He hung there for several minutes, trying to pull himself up, but unable to do so because of the awkwardness and bulk of the life preserver. He dared not take it off; a sea might catch him and carry him away even as he struggled to remove the vest. So he hung by the rope, tiring in the battering of the sea.

Finally, as Greene's strength gave out, he dropped the rope and allowed himself to drift. The current carried him back,

back near the bow of *Vandalia,* not close enough to catch hold of any projection from the ship, but close enough so that he was able to grasp a piece of flotsam, to which he clung with all his strength. Now he drifted back and forth in the white foaming water in the lee of the wreck of his ship.

Ashore, Consul Blacklock and Chief Seumanu Tafa and the officers of the *Nipsic* saw Chief Engineer Greene's struggle for life. The Samoans formed a new human chain that stretched far out into the current, as far as a man could stand.

There they waited.

Soon Chief Engineer Greene was carried around the stern of *Vandalia* and into the swift current that flowed along the side of the reef. He could be seen clearly enough, clutching his piece of wreckage for dear life, holding his head above the waves, as the current brought him in a long sweep inshore. Had there been nothing to stop him, the Chief Engineer would have come in along the shore, then would have been carried parallel to it, and—unless he could break the hold and swim in himself—he would then have been captured by the current of the Vaisingano and sped out to a cold sea that would have cast his body up perhaps five miles away.

But Seumanu Tafa's men were there, and as the Chief Engineer swung past, they grasped him and hustled him ashore. In ten minutes he was being rubbed down in a cheery warm room in the American consulate, while the storm raged over his mates outside.

On the mainmast of the *Vandalia,* Cadet Wiley weighed his chances of survival and did not find them good. He wondered how long the masts would stand the tremendous pounding of the sea and wind. Although he was a husky youth, the water lashed against his body so forcefully that it had already numbed him. He was hungry and exhausted, battered and bruised. He wondered how long he could hold out on the mast and decided that he had enough strength to try the swim to the *Nipsic* at this time, but might not have it later. He would try.

Cadet Wiley worked himself out on the mast to a position near Ensign John H. Gibbons, a particular friend. They talked it over. If they could make the *Nipsic*, they would be safe, and they might be able to get a line back to the *Vandalia* to help the others.

As they watched, several seamen let go their perches and leaped into the sea, trying to do the same. The trouble, they could see, was that the *Nipsic* was not directly to leeward—there was an open stretch of water where the seas had full sweep, and this water was clogged with wreckage. While they watched, one swimmer after another struck out hopefully for the *Nipsic*, was battered by the wreckage, and sank, or seemed almost to reach the *Nipsic*'s stern, then was swept around, out of reach, and disappeared in the green foam.

Gibbons and Wiley agreed that the chance was worth the taking.

"But, Henry, my boy," said Ensign Gibbons, "I can't make it. I haven't got the strength. I must stick by the ship and take my chances."

"Well," said Cadet Wiley, "good luck. I'm going."

"You'll make it," said Gibbons, with an encouragement he could scarcely have felt. "God bless your efforts."

The *Vandalia*'s main yard was lashed across the rail. Cadet Wiley took off all his clothing and then made his way to the starboard main yardarm. He stood up on the yardarm, waved goodbye to Ensign Gibbons, and plunged overboard.

Cadet Wiley was young and strong, and after a terrible bout with the sea, he managed to reach the *Nipsic*. He grabbed a piece of rigging that hung over the side of the ship and tried to pull himself up, but the long swim had exhausted him, and he could not get up, so he hung, between safety and the sea.

"I don't know how long I hung there," he said later, "but it seemed like an eternity. I think the line I had was wire. I could have hung on for a long time in still water, but this was different. *Bang!* would go a heavy sea against the side, and I would go bang with it. At the same time I would go hand over hand up the line I was holding. Then out would go the sea, and down I would slide. Each time I had my head out of water long enough to yell, I would sing out, hoping that someone on board would hear me and haul me on board. But there was no one on board." (Because the *Nipsic*'s men would not come back to try to save their comrades.)

After a few minutes of banging against the side of the *Nipsic,* young Wiley was growing weak. He had been hit on the head by a piece of wreckage during his swim, his hands were cut from the wire, and his strength was leaving him. He hung on, his life racing before him, thinking of the things he had done that he ought not to have done, and the things undone that he ought to have done, worrying about the message he might have left for his mother and father. He was tortured by his sins. He was tortured by the wire rope in his hands. He was tortured by the battering, and the sickness of salt water taken through the mouth in large quantities. Eventually—five minutes later—he decided to end the torture, and he let go, intending to drown himself.

But drowning was not a voluntary act. Cadet Wiley struggled in the water, and as he struggled, he found himself alongside a heavy wooden ladder that had floated off one of the ships. He grabbed the ladder and clung to it.

As the ladder drifted in the current, sometimes it turned end over end, and then Cadet Wiley had to climb back aboard. He was too far gone to notice what was happening, but he was drifting inshore, and yet at an angle, so that it was touch and go as to whether he would come to the shore or would be caught, with his ladder, by the current of the Vaisingano, which would sweep him down the center of the harbor raceway and out to sea.

This danger was apparent to the Samoans ashore, who grouped themselves around the edge of the current and ran a chain out as far as they could go. Two Samoans went too far in their efforts to save the stricken one—they were caught in the current and swept out to sea—but there were others there to take their places, and just as Wiley's ladder seemed to make up its mind to go to the Vaisingano and destruction, a Samoan grasped a rung and hauled it in, so that others might take the ladder and its human burden and haul it swiftly in to shore and safety.

Young Wiley was completely unconscious when they lifted him off the ladder, although he had held on until that very moment. He remembered nothing as they brought him to the American consulate. He revived for a few minutes as Surgeon Derr and his assistants rolled the water out of him, and then he lapsed back into unconsciousness.

CHAPTER SIXTEEN

Day of Death—Evening

IT SEEMED the day would never end. Rain poured down in a continual torrent, the spindrift between the seas flew in sheets, and every few minutes a wave so high that it towered above the mastheads of the *Vandalia* engulfed the ship and its unhappy crew. As the wave came down, every man held his breath, renewed his grip on whatever he was holding, and waited, praying or cursing, while the sea swept over him.

When noon passed, no man knew it, for the sun was invisible and there was no indication of time. Hour followed hour, marked only by the regular coming of the huge waves, each of which tested every man, each of which brought every man closer to exhaustion.

On the foremast where Engineer Webster and his men huddled, First Class Fireman Joseph Griffin seemed to lose his will to live. As the sea swept over them with ever greater force, it seemed, Griffin complained, then became dazed. Finally, in a lull between waves he turned and spoke to Webster.

"The next sea that comes," Griffin said quietly, "I am going to let go."

A few minutes later the next comber broke over the ship, and when it had passed, Fireman Griffin was gone. He was not seen again.

Elsewhere on the *Vandalia* men began dropping off the rigging, one by one; four Chinese cooks and one landsman slipped away; one other, Ah Kee, a wardroom mess boy, had attempted earlier to save Paymaster Arms, without success, but he did manage to hold on to his perch above the poop, although he weighed less than a hundred pounds. The Marines suffered most; they lost fifteen men to the sea that day, fighting men who were unused to long hours of clinging in the ship's rigging.

Shortly after noon, Seaman C. W. Johnson made a gallant attempt to carry a line to the *Nipsic,* but was forced back and nearly lost his life before his companions could rescue him by pulling in the line he was carrying. An hour later, a seaman swam with a line to the *Nipsic,* and then men began crossing to that ship; Boatswain's Mate George Murrage went; and so did William Brown, the first quartermaster, and a coal-heaver named William Howat. They were the first to go, and the first to be lost on that perilous crossing. A dozen others followed and made it safely, then half a dozen other men were on the line when an unusually ferocious sea swept them all away. Lieutenant Carlin watched them go and put a stop to the use of the line to the *Nipsic;* it was too dangerous a passage.

With the *Nipsic* escape avenue closed, the men began to lose heart, and seeing this, Lieutenant Carlin allowed Seaman E. M. Hammar to try to carry a line to shore. Hammar had volunteered and had pressed his case, but it was only when there seemed to be no other hope that Carlin would permit him to make the attempt.

Hammar struck out, the line tied around his waist. He had not gone three strokes when a surging undertow caught him, brought him back to the *Vandalia,* and smashed his head against the side of the ship. He was dead and gone.

Other men were ready to volunteer, and three others tried; not one could get through the wreckage. Seaman William Fooye came to Lieutenant Carlin and asked that he be allowed to try, but after four attempts Carlin saw that it was useless and forbade another effort. The men would have to stick with the ship until the gale dropped and they could have help from shore.

What a decision for an officer to have to make! Around him, Carlin could see the signs of exhaustion, and occasionally he saw a man steel himself and jump, rather than take any more of the pounding of the sea.

With the heavy seas, the wreckage became a terrible hazard. Flotsam swept over the ship as if shot out of a cannon, and when a piece struck a man, he was washed overboard, stunned, or killed. Carlin considered the chances of getting a line ashore by buoy, and several volunteers went down to the decks below, secured buoys, and made the attempt to throw them so they would drift inshore with a line. The buoys moved temptingly in toward the shore, then swung around and carried the lines out to sea. Pulled back, they repeated the performance, until Lieutenant Carlin told his men to save their strength for the ordeal ahead.

Once, during the afternoon, *Vandalia* swung around close to *Nipsic,* so that the *Vandalia*'s foreyard on the forecastle came close to *Nipsic,* and finally the starboard end of the foreyard touched the smaller ship. Had the crew of *Nipsic* been aboard the ship trying to save lives, many men might have escaped in the brief time the ships were together.

But the *Nipsic* was a ghost ship. *Vandalia*'s Second Class

Fireman Apostola Callarito left his perch on the foremast and made his way aboard the *Nipsic*. Immediately he began to let down ladders, ropes, and boatswain's chairs to save lives. Seeing the first real chance of safety, a number of men made their way across. From the shore an American resident named Vickering saw Callarito on the *Nipsic* and joined him there to help save the others. He and Callarito managed to pass a line to *Vandalia*, and a hawser was made fast to the foremast. The men hoped to rig a breeches buoy between the ships, but the *Vandalia* swung away. The hawser was paid out to its full length; *Vandalia* swung back and slackened the hawser so it fell into the sea; the men aboard *Nipsic* took in the slack; thus the contest went, with the hawser moving up and down, back and forth, giving the would-be rescuers no opportunity to rig their life-saving apparatus; finally, as if tired of the game, *Vandalia* swung away and the hawser snapped in two.

Men continued to slip off the lee side of *Vandalia;* a man's will to live seemed to be all that differentiated the survivors from those who died. One seaman was swept overboard twice by the sea, but each time succeeded in clutching some of the cordage that hung down from the foreyard and crawled back aboard. Others simply gave up and sank quietly.

By midafternoon the after part of *Vandalia* began to break up under the pounding. The ship's back was broken, which accounted for her comparative stability, even though the after end of the ship was taking a frightful beating. The cabin was gutted, and the poop deck trembled as though it would break loose from the ship—and finally did so. With every surge the masts moved as if to unseat themselves from the keelson, sending chills through the men who clung to them for life. The body of a drowned man washed up on the bridge, just forward of the smokestack, and one of the body's arms became entangled in the stanchion. So for an hour this corpse swung to and from its horrible gibbet, reminding the men on the foremast how close they were to death, until a particularly heavy sea tore the body adrift and it disappeared over the rail.

Occasionally, during this afternoon of terror, the men of *Vandalia* would take heart at a lull in the gale or as a tiny patch of lighter cloud showed through the darker gray. But each lull in the wind would be followed by a stronger blast, each quieting of the sea by a greater wave, each patch of light by a darkening of the greasy black sky.

The water was warm enough, and the actual temperature was in the eighties, but the men had been exposed to the sea for so long that the heat had gone from their bodies. Every time a sea passed over them, they began to chatter with the cold. The wave would go by, the chattering would continue, then die down, only to be revived by the next wave. Men were suffering and men were dying, but they were doing so in almost complete silence. From the beginning, except for the occasional conversation or exchange of information between Lieutenant Carlin and the others, there was no sound but the sounds of the storm. No man who went down died with a cry on his lips. There were no shouts of fear or defiance from the men huddled on the spars. All that could be heard was the roar of the wind, the crash of the waves, and the hissing of the foam as it washed over them.

By three o'clock in the afternoon, the broken ship was resting solidly on the bottom, with only the after part of the poop deck and the forward part of the forecastle showing. When the poop deck carried away, all that could be seen of the ship was the forecastle, with the masts rising straight up out of the water.

Lieutenant Carlin had climbed into the mizzentop, where

he sat, exhausted, his legs dropping through the opening in the platform.

Soon after the *Calliope* passed *Trenton* and went out to sea and safety, the flagship's condition became desperate. Admiral Kimberly lost hope that he could save the ship.

"If we have to go down," he told Captain Farquhar, "let us do so with our flag flying."

So the storm ensign was hoisted on the mizzen gaff, and *Trenton* showed her defiance of the elements.

As the afternoon wore on, the *Trenton* continued to drag toward the inner edge of the reef. Then the wind hauled around to the west, which brought pressure of a different kind: at three o'clock the port sheet chain parted, and within the hour the starboard bower was gone. Captain Farquhar ordered the ship veered to 90 fathoms on the remaining anchor, but one anchor was not likely to save them for long, and every man aboard the flagship knew it.

Trenton was pushed back across the harbor by the changing wind and threatened to go ashore on the eastern reef. As she dragged, she came almost up on the wreck of the *Peter Godeffroy* and would have struck that hulk, had not the bark dragged just as *Trenton* approached her.

During this drifting, Admiral Kimberly, Captain Farquhar, and Lieutenant Brown were on the poop deck of the flagship. The command was the Captain's, but it was traditional for him to tell the officer of the deck his wishes and let the orders be issued by the subordinate. Admiral Kimberly did not interfere except when he felt he must in the interest of the ship and crew.

It was impossible to set enough canvas to steer the ship or even to help save her, but Lieutenant Brown did have one idea: he conferred with his seniors, and they agreed that it was worth trying, so he ordered all hands aft into the mizzen rigging to create a sort of human sail that would catch the wind and help the ship off the reef by keeping her head into the wind.

Cadet R. H. Jackson heard the order and led the way with a cheer. In a moment the men were swarming up the ratlines, and soon the effect could be felt. The ship had been bearing down broadside onto the eastern reef; she turned into the wind, and only her stern was threatened.

The *Trenton* moved ever closer to the reef, until her taffrail actually overhung the coral on one surge of the sea as she pulled against her single remaining anchor. At this point, Lieutenant Brown urgently requested permission to slip the cable, hoping to turn the ship and bring her alongside the reef into the sandy beach. Captain Farquhar had great confidence in Lieutenant Brown's seamanship, but Admiral Kimberly stepped in and stopped the move. To slip the cable then, said the Admiral, would be to lose the ship. The fall and rush of the water would tend to keep the ship off the reef. They must have patience.

The *Trenton* drifted along the eastern reef, saved because the reef sloped gradually to the east; as the flagship was blown by wind from the north and west and kept her head into the wind, she came slipping alongside the reef without touching.

As the ship moved inshore, the water became smoother in this eastern end of the harbor, and the single anchor seemed to hold much better than it had before. But a new danger threatened: the drift of *Trenton* brought her down into the hawse of *Olga*.

Of all the ships in the harbor, *Olga* had taken the storm the best. She was riding well to her anchors, although she pitched heavily and porpoised in the seas on her long chains. Her engines never faltered, and if any vessel seemed likely to survive this day, it was she. Captain von Erhardt had shown superb seamanship all day long and gave no evidence of its deserting him at this point. As the hulk called *Trenton* drifted helplessly down on *Olga*, the Captain reversed his engines and escaped her lunge.

Admiral Kimberly suggested that the 8-inch rifle from the forecastle of *Trenton* be jettisoned with a 10-inch hawser attached, to help the single anchor hold and thus prevent a recurrence of the near-accident. It was done, but too late— the *Trenton* was caught in a titanic sea and surged toward the German vessel. Again Captain von Erhardt saw her coming, and this time he turned his rudder hard to port and by using every bit of power managed again to avoid the helpless American ship.

A third time the *Trenton* drifted down, and this time Captain von Erhardt could not stop her. The bow of *Olga* came over the port quarter of *Trenton,* carrying away the boats there, snapping the standing and running rigging and taking off the quarter gallery.

Back the *Olga* went, to the end of her chains, but again Trenton came down on her sloppily, this time presenting her starboard quarter. It was a harder smash; *Olga*'s bowsprit and figurehead came in across the quarter, snapping off the lines that held the storm ensign and dropping that ensign down on the German ship's forecastle, where it curled around the foremast. The starboard boats of *Trenton* were smashed, and her starboard quarter gallery was gone, but the hull was relatively unhurt—for the moment.

Captain von Erhardt saw that unless he could move away he must smash *Trenton* again and again, until real damage was done to both ships. So it was time to take drastic action.

He ordered full steam and the slipping of the three anchor chains. He turned hard to starboard, and sped his ship toward the mud flat on the eastern shore, just below the point where the reef came to an end. Had *Trenton* been on his other side, he might have tried to run out of the harbor, but he could not; to avoid disaster he was forced to beach his ship. Captain Douglas, who had climbed aboard the *Olga* after his ship was run down by *Nipsic*, knew where to go, and he instructed the German. Beach her they did; *Olga*'s engines responded without a lull or a screech, and she slid smoothly into the soft mud in the safety of the inner bay. Captain von Erhardt kept the engines running until he was sure his ship was hard aground, then had them shut off, and she stood, safe on the western shore of Matautu, stern to the sea so that the wind and waves drove her steadily bow in to shore.

Shortly after the collisions with *Olga*, the American flagship was captured by the current of the Vaisingano, which swung her around and sent her moving toward the center of the harbor. Soon *Trenton* was dragging astern toward the western reef and in the grip of the current that bore inward along the lip of that reef.

Then she began dragging down on *Vandalia*.

CHAPTER SEVENTEEN

Moment of Hope

AN HOUR before dark the men of *Vandalia* could see *Trenton* coming toward them, borne inexorably by the current along the reef. There was no question of the final result: *Trenton* would drag in on *Vandalia* and strike her, and when the flagship struck the smaller vessel with her tremendous weight, the *Vandalia's* weakened masts would pop out of the keelson, the men would be catapulted into the water or crushed between the hulls of the two ships, and that would be the end.

Numbed, dazed, exhausted, the men of *Vandalia* clutched their slender handholds on life and watched.

The darkness of the storm was augmented suddenly by a darker black, which meant that the tropical night had descended with the finality nature employs as the sun drops sizzling into the sea. Having seen *Trenton*, the men of the *Vandalia* could trace her darker shadow against the clouds as she moved inward, and a few twinkling lights on the flagship made her passage even clearer. Slowly, the *Trenton* came in, doing all she could to avoid the issue. The storm, mizzen, and mizzen staysails were set, with sheets amidships to prevent the ship from sheering. The reef remained directly under the *Trenton*'s stern as she came down the harbor, and the men of *Trenton* rolled their anxious eyes from reef to shore, watching the distance diminish. At six o'clock *Trenton* was two hundred fifty feet from *Vandalia;* an hour later, she was only two hundred feet away, and then she began moving faster in the increasing current along the reef.

From his perch in the mizzen top, Lieutenant Carlin could see that *Trenton*'s stern would soon strike *Vandalia*'s port beam. He ordered the men around him to move down the rigging and make ready to leap for life when the ships struck, before the masts toppled out of her. Seeing his movement down, the men in the main and foremast rigging did the same.

Trenton's distance was one hundred feet, and then seventy-five feet. The men of *Vandalia* watched wearily as their destroyer came at them.

Suddenly, a cheer broke across the water—the men of *Trenton* were cheering the men of *Vandalia,* those hundred poor souls who, naked and forlorn, clung to the ropes and wires of their stricken ship. And then, more than cheering, the band of the flagship struck up the "Star-Spangled Banner," and through the darkness of the night a thousand persons aship and ashore heard the stirring anthem of the Republic of North America, over the howling of the storm.

Admiral Kimberly was giving his men their due.

The Admiral was in charge, and Captain Farquhar was his willing aide in this gallantry. But it was not gallantry alone; the Admiral could imagine the mental and physical condition of the men who had stood and clung all day aboard that ship, bruised and battered, their flesh cut by ropes and wires and their eyes blinded by salt spray. The men of *Vandalia* had not eaten or drunk for more than twenty-four hours; since morning, when Engineer Webster had secured the whisky from the dispensary, they had not had stimulation of any kind. Now, to give the men impetus in their fight for life, the Admiral brought them stimulant of another kind— all he could give them.

Aboard the *Vandalia* the response was all the Admiral could have asked. From a hundred parched throats came a faint responsive cheer. The castaways had taken heart. From the shore the watchers noted the faintness of the *Vandalia* cheer, more than the cheer itself.

"God help them," said one watcher to another.

The officers of *Nipsic* and those few shamefaced crew members who had been persuaded to come and help their fellow Americans heard the cheering and the music first with surprise, then with awe, and finally with determination that aroused new vigor in them. Lieutenant Shearman and Ensigns Purcell and Jones found a boat and prepared to man it. A handful of the men of the *Nipsic* awkwardly volunteered to go along. They were ready to launch when they looked into the sea and saw that their little boat could not possibly live in the gale. Impatiently they waited for the moment when they could show their spirit to their comrades.

Ensign Field was no longer with them; he had collapsed on the beach at four o'clock in the afternoon and had been carried to the American consulate, where he now lay, wracked with high fever, and unconscious. On the foremast of the *Vandalia*, Engineer Webster was weeping unashamedly; for the first time since noon, he had hope that he would live again.

Aboard the *Trenton*, Admiral Kimberly was determined that his men would be saved. As the ships came near enough so the men on *Vandalia* could see the figures in the rigging and at the rails of the flagship, preparations were being made. Just before eight o'clock, *Trenton*'s stern struck *Vandalia* abeam, and at that moment the Admiral ordered the firing of rockets, carrying light lines over the three masts of *Vandalia*. In a moment the lines were secured, and a hawser was made fast to the foretopmast ahead. Just after eight o'clock, the *Trenton* began to swing around, coming nearly parallel to the *Vandalia*, the sterns almost touching and the bows separated by forty feet.

As the ships touched, the men in the mizzen and main rigging of the *Vandalia* began jumping and scrambling their way to the flagship. They crawled out onto the yards and jumped for the deck—and just in time they were, too, for in a few moments the starboard quarter of *Trenton* smashed heavily into the port quarter of *Vandalia*, and the mizzenmast toppled over into the sea on the leeward side. Among those to spring for the deck at that moment was Lieutenant Carlin; he watched, glancing backward as some of his men tumbled to their deaths, to be crushed between the two vessels.

Trenton swung around, her bottom touching the sand, her stern first grazing the reef and then the wreckage of an inter-island schooner. When the hawser was secured on the fore-mast, some of the sailors began going hand-over-hand across to the safety of the flagship. Engineer Webster tried that route, but found that he had not the strength. He abandoned the perch he had held all day and climbed into the port fore rigging; there he waited.

The officers of the *Trenton* had been prepared to take to the rigging of their ship, but they discovered that *Vandalia* gave the *Trenton* a certain protection from the fury of the sea and wind, and they concentrated on the rescue of the *Vandalia* men in the foremast rigging.

At 8:30 *Trenton* sailors began throwing ropes into the rigging of *Vandalia*. One of the first to catch a line was Chief Boatswain Winchester.

"Here's a chance for you, boys," he shouted, and showed

his frightened men the way by swinging himself across to the deck of the flagship.

Engineer Webster was feeling very shaky, but he thought he might manage to swing across in a similar manner, and he dropped down from his place in the rigging to the end of the yard. Webster signaled, and a line was thrown; he caught the bight and swung himself out. But Engineer Webster was too weak to make the deck; he swung against the side of the *Trenton* at the water's edge and struck there so violently that he wondered whether he had broken any bones. He could not draw himself up, nor could he hang there long without falling into the water; and if he fell, he knew he would never have the strength to get out of the water again.

Engineer Webster cried out, and someone heard. The line was raised, he on the end, and he was able to pull himself astride the torpedo boom. Helped by a coal-heaver from his own ship, Webster then climbed up through the starboard fore chains, slowly and painfully, and stepped over the low forecastle rail of the *Trenton*; thereupon he collapsed to the deck and lay there for some time unable to move or speak. Yet fifteen minutes later, he suddenly realized in safety that he had been twenty-six and a half hours without food or drink, except for two ounces of whisky.

Dr. Cordeiro, who was in the foretop, was not as fortunate as Engineer Webster. When the surgeon climbed out on the foreyard, he slipped and fell and struck some submerged object on the deck of the *Vandalia* with force enough to dislocate his kneecap. Worse, he was thrown into the water, and the waves closed around him. Yet somehow he managed to grasp a line and was pulled up onto the *Trenton*.

Those who could be saved from the mizzen had been saved; most of those on the foremast were saved, but still more than a score of men remained aboard the *Vandalia,* clinging to the mainmast and its rigging.

The rescue work continued.

The men in the main lowered themselves to safety with little more than rope burns.

Lieutenant J. C. Wilson was not so lucky. Lieutenant Wilson was perched in the maintop, where he had sought refuge early in the day, and at nine o'clock he began making his way down. Wilson crawled out onto the yard and prepared to leap for the deck of the *Trenton*, but lost his footing and fell twenty feet into the water between the hulls of the two ships. He was washed back aboard the *Vandalia*, submerged as she was.

Wilson managed to catch hold of the Jacob's ladder that ran up and down the after part of the *Vandalia*'s mainmast and tried to climb up, but was too weak to do more than bring his head above the surface. There he clung, between life and death, with no one to watch him die. His ship was entirely submerged, not even the forecastle standing out of water, and the waves were breaking over his head every few seconds.

He was sure he was lost.

At this point the *Trenton* drifted down on the *Vandalia*'s wreck until *Trenton*'s stern was pressing hard against the *Vandalia*'s main yard. The yard must soon yield to the pressure and fall away, and then the mast would go a few moments later. Even stuck to the bottom by the weight of thousands of tons of water, the wreck of the *Vandalia* was rolling violently. Had any of the rescuers seen Lieutenant Wilson in his peril, it would seem unlikely that they would have risked their lives so uselessly as to try to save him.

But one aboard *Trenton* did see—Cabin Steward Fuji Hachitaro. Without hesitation, Steward Hachitaro climbed over the stern of the *Trenton* and onto the main yard of the *Vandalia*, then teetered along that perilous walkway until he could reach the Lieutenant. The small Oriental pulled the big Caucasian up the Jacob's ladder and along the yard, back into the rigging. From the *Trenton* a line was thrown, and Hachitaro secured this around the body of the half-conscious Lieutenant, under the arms, and the men on the *Trenton* hauled Lieutenant Wilson aboard. Steward Hachitaro stood on the quivering yard, his life in peril every moment, and waited calmly for the rope to be thrown back for him. It was. He swung aboard the *Trenton*.

A few minutes later the *Vandalia*'s mainmast fell, killing several men who were still clinging to the rigging.

Ensign Ripley was standing on the *Vandalia*'s main yard as the mast began to go. He jumped into the sea on the leeward side of the wreck and was swept over the hull of the *Nipsic*. He was able to grasp a line hanging down from the *Nipsic*'s deck, but he could not pull himself up, so he abandoned the line and seized a piece of floating wreckage. Soon Ensign Ripley saw that the wreckage was going nowhere and that he must swim against the outbound current if he was to save himself, so he pushed away the wreckage and swam for his life. He escaped the current and made the shore, but so completely exhausted was he that he sank down on the sand and was being drawn back out by the undertow when he was sighted by Lieutenant Shearman and Ensign Purcell, on their patrol of the beach, looking for survivors. The two tired officers saw, they came, they dragged Ripley out of the water and turned him over to men who carried the youngster to the warmth of the American consulate.

CHAPTER EIGHTEEN

Day of Reckoning

ALL NIGHT long the storm continued to blow at hurricane force, the wind holding almost at due north during the early part of the night, then shifting to the west just before the beginning of the middle watch.

After the survivors were transferred from *Vandalia* to *Trenton*, Admiral Kimberly and his officers could consider their best chances of ensuring survival of ship and crew. The *Trenton* rode uneasily, lying alongside *Vandalia*, secured by the 10-inch hawser around the wreck's foremast and her own starboard sheet anchor. The *Vandalia* was better than an anchor, so fast was she to the sands with the full weight of the sea inside her, but no one knew how long her foremast would stand fixed to the keelson. Captain Farquhar ordered another hawser put around the wreck's foremast, and using all available manpower hauled *Trenton* inshore slightly, improving her riding.

The officers and men of *Trenton* spelled each other on the hand pumps. The pumping never stopped, and yet it seemed so hopeless; gradually, indomitably, the sea gained on the sailors, and the water rose ever higher in the compartments below *Trenton*'s decks. The depth was six feet, and soon it was seven feet, then eight.

Those who were not pumping tried to help the half-dead survivors of the *Vandalia*, who were sprawled about on *Trenton*'s deck in places to shelter them from the worst biting of the storm.

Every inch of deck was dripping with seawater; every man was wet through. *Trenton*'s fresh-water tanks had been fouled by the sea, and the fires in the galley had been out for more than twenty-four hours; all the food available for the men of *Vandalia*, as for those of *Trenton*, was a few bits of sodden hardtack.

This night, seas came pouring over the port hammock rail of *Trenton*, sousing her from one end to the other, spray shooting as high as the crosstrees and extending over to the wreck of *Vandalia*.

The storm was growing worse; as the water increased, more men were called aft to man the pumps, and they went gladly; the men did not know they were trying to pump the ocean dry—the collision with the reef had battered a large hole in *Trenton*'s stern below the water line, and there was no hope of stopping the entrance of the sea. The situation of *Trenton* was not desperate, but it was hopeless, and as the water level kept rising slowly, every man began to sense that this was so.

For some time after Engineer Webster was carried to a fairly dry spot near the main hatch, he lay there regaining his strength until suddenly the need for water and food overcame his physical exhaustion, and he arose and climbed down the hatch.

He crossed the gun deck and passed the Admiral's pantry, where he was recognized by Ah Fat, the steward, with whom he had served three years before, when the Chinese cook was aboard the *Iroquois*.

"Hello, Mist' Lebs. You all right? S'pose you hungry?"

Webster was ready to embrace the steward. Hungry! he said, he was starving and dying of thirst.

Ah Fat opened a can of mutton, found some dry hardtack, and—best of all—poured a glass of fresh, clear water from the small store left in the Admiral's cooler.

Ah Fat disappeared then, but returned in a few minutes carrying a pair of Chinese pajamas and clean underwear, so that Engineer Webster could change clothing from the skin out. As he changed, he examined his shirt and trousers for the first time: every fiber was filled with mud and sand that had been forced into the material by the wind in ten hours of buffeting by the storm.

After changing, Engineer Webster went into the ward-room, where he saw Lieutenants Carlin and Wilson and Ensign Gibbons; Carlin and Ensign Gibbons were sitting in chairs, battered and bruised; Lieutenant Wilson, who had so nearly lost his life in trying to escape from the wreck, was lying on a lounge at the after end of the cabin, retching violently.

Sometime shortly before midnight, the storm seemed to reach a height of fury. The sea smashed against the *Trenton* with such force that she groaned and moaned in every timber. The deck pumps thudded and thumped away, gaining nothing, and the waves thundered against the oaken sides of the ship. Engineer Webster was asleep on the deck in the ward-room when he was awakened by the simultaneous surge of the ship as she was struck by a giant wave, the rattle of a sea on deck, the screech of the cabin air port as it was torn from its fastenings, and the unwelcome drenching of the warm sea that came pouring into the cabin.

By midnight, the barometer had begun to rise again; at the beginning of the middle watch, it reached 29.52 inches; the center of the storm had passed away to the north, and, this time, finally. By three o'clock in the morning, the sailors aboard the *Trenton* could tell the difference; the pounding decreased, wave after wave, the wind's force became less cutting, and the noises of the sea and air gradually decreased. *Trenton* began to ride more easily, although the men made no gains in their battle with the sea by pump and bucket, but by five o'clock in the morning, the wind had abated, although the sea continued rough.

During the night most of the Samoans and Americans had gone from the shore to try to get some sleep, although Lieutenant Shearman and Ensign Purcell continued to patrol the beach with a handful of men; before dawn broke, the lights came on in Apia, and the people moved back to the shore to attempt a rescue that was deemed possible.

Chief Seumanu Tafa took out the first boat himself, leaving before dawn had actually broken. The sea was very rough, and the current of the reef and the Vaisingano continued treacherous, but his great brown outrigger canoe bounced across the waves and managed to reach the bow of the *Trenton* carrying a light line from shore. The men of *Trenton* handed a 10-inch hawser down to the canoe, and Seumanu Tafa and his paddlers moved back to shore, where they and the hawser were grasped by willing hands and the big rope was made fast. In a few minutes, boats went out from shore, and as the morning dawned, four more hawsers were stretched from ship to land.

The Samoans in their boats began the rescue of the men of *Trenton* and *Vandalia*. First to come ashore were the injured men of both ships, and then the entire crew of *Vandalia,* many of whom had suffered broken arms and legs; scarcely an officer or man from the sunken ship could walk unassisted to the American consulate, where they were all taken for examination and treatment.

As the gale died down, Admiral Kimberly and Captain

Farquhar ordered the examination of the *Trenton* to ascertain her seaworthiness. The Admiral had kept the pumps going all night in the hope that the ship might be hauled off the sand when the storm ended. As dawn came and he could see the damage, the story of the storm emerged. The propeller was gone. The rudder was wrecked. The ship had settled hard on the bottom and had broken her back in two places, abreast the mizzenmast and near the smokestack. Because of the hole (which could not be seen in this early inspection), the water was up to the engine-room platform and still rising.

As always, the next decision was the Admiral's, as senior officer. Should he try to save the ship, or abandon her? The word *abandon* was one to make a naval officer writhe, for it meant the end of an association; disregarding the possible complications of abandonment on an officer's career, he could never forget a ship of his command, and to abandon one was somehow to consign a friend to death.

Yet, there was no saving *Trenton,* and the Admiral made his difficult decision. He told Captain Farquhar they would abandon ship.

The Captain ordered up the ship's stores that could be salvaged from the water; the Paymaster's safe was sent ashore; and the ship's available supply of rifles and ammunition was broken out and sent ashore under careful guard—the Admiral now had again begun to consider the political situation he faced in Apia.

Early in the morning, Commander Mullan of *Nipsic* came aboard to see the Admiral and received a thorough dressing-down for abandoning his ship and his comrades to the storm. There was no excuse, there could not be one, and in the light of this morning the action seemed nearly criminal. No great calm had settled over the harbor, nor was the sun shining down warm and radiant, but a gentle breeze was blowing from the north, and the overcast sky with occasional glimpses of light gray and blue was a welcome relief from the gale that had lasted nearly two full days. *Nipsic* was high and dry, but compared to the other ships in the harbor, she seemed relatively undamaged. Not a hull remained afloat! *Eber* had vanished, along with a dozen merchantmen of various sizes; all that could be seen of her was her ornamental bow and figurehead, washed up on shore. *Adler* lay on her beam ends, the Samoans at work with line and boats to take the forty survivors off, moving among great blocks of coral that had broken off from the reef. *Olga*'s crew were coming away in some of her own boats, helped by other boats from the shore. *Vandalia* seemed to be only a mast and a forecastle sticking out of the water, and *Trenton* lay crookedly beside her. The shore was filled with wreckage, and the Samoans and civilians were trundling dead bodies back to shelter for laying out and burial in the French and British cemeteries.

Admiral Kimberly, looking out on the scene and looking at Commander Mullan, was not pleased.

The commander of the *Nipsic* was ordered back aboard his ship, to take stock and report to the Admiral on his ship's condition and the chances of bringing her off the beach. At 9:30 that morning, the Captain and his officers returned to the ship with such members of the crew as could be rounded up at that time; many of the crew were disheveled and dirty, and many men were scarcely sober after their day and night of debauchery ashore. The men of the *Vandalia* and the *Trenton* were sore and sick and weary, but the men of the *Nipsic* were the sorriest crew of all; they wore the badge of dishonor, and they knew it.

Captain Mullan's first move—which should have been taken nearly twenty-four hours earlier—was to sound off the stern. Ten feet of water was discovered, and the next move was to secure what was left of the starboard bower chain to a tree ashore, to prevent the ship from washing off into deep water.

Next, Captain Mullan's men sounded the well and found twenty-four inches of water in it. Engineer Hall set the bilge pumps going, and men with hand pumps and buckets were sent down to the magazine to take out the four inches of water sloshing on the deck.

It soon became apparent just how wild the *Nipsic*'s crew had become, and how accessible the ship had been all day long to determined men from shore: someone who knew the ship—some shipmate—had been aboard during the day or night and had forced locks, opened bags, and stolen valuables from the cabins of the officers and the lockers of the men.

King Mataafa came down to the harbor that morning, having word of the total disaster, and directed the Samoans in their work of saving the crews of *all* ships, American and German. He then went to the American consulate and offered his services to Consul Blacklock, to whatever end they might be used.

The consulate to which he went was as disorganized as a madhouse; all night long, rescued sailors had been brought into the consulate, and that building could not possibly accommodate them all. The recovered men were told that they would have to leave and find shelter elsewhere, so the injured could be treated by Dr. Derr and his helpers; the men straggled out and found what shelter they could, too often in the saloons, then returned, like homing pigeons.

Aboard the *Trenton* in the morning hours, the Admiral ordered the flagship's band to duty, and as the crew labored to bring up stores and the men of the *Vandalia* were sent ashore in boat after boat, their senses were livened by the sounds of "Hail, Columbia" and a dozen marches.

In this midmorning hour, Admiral Kimberly had to map out a plan and create order from the chaos that he knew existed ashore. He did not yet know the full story of the crew of the *Nipsic*, but it was apparent that with several hundred

American and German sailors on the beach the danger of some incident was very great.

The Admiral's first problem was to secure accommodations for the officers and men of the *Vandalia*. Admiral Kimberly appointed Engineer Webster acting paymaster of the *Vandalia* and ordered him ashore to make arrangements for the shelter and messing of his ship's men.

All morning long, boats had been moving back and forth between the shore and *Trenton,* and now, when Chief Seumanu Tafa came alongside at the steering oar of his great canoe, Webster was lowered into the boat by rope and sent ashore. The Chief guided the boat along the starboard side of *Vandalia,* and as they passed the ship, Webster could see that the storm had enjoyed its little joke on mere mankind: the poop deck, torn away from the stern, had played about until it had come to rest atop the topgallant forecastle at the opposite end of the ship.

Engineer Webster was landed easily enough—the waves of the day before were gone, and there was not even a noticeable surf running in the harbor inside the reef. On shore Webster was warmly greeted by Lieutenant Shearman and several other officers of the *Nipsic,* who were still patrolling the beach, and by most of the people of Apia, who had come to stare at the wreckage of the storm. A dozen times, as he made his way to Apia, Engineer Webster was stopped by Europeans and natives, all expressing their sorrow at the death and disaster that had been wreaked upon their harbor. There was no looting, there was no desire for personal gain; the people of Apia came to the beach to sympathize and help and caused little trouble to the military police of two countries who stood guard.

Mr. Gurr, an English businessman, took Engineer Webster to his general store and soon had the young officer clothed in a pair of cotton trousers, a high-necked Chinese blouse, canvas shoes, and a straw hat. Then Webster set out to find shelter and food for the men of the *Vandalia;* before noon he had made arrangements to use the copra warehouse of the MacArthur company as a barracks; it would take a day or so to make it ready, so temporary quarters were arranged in the Evangelical Church building near the American consulate. Food would be supplied on a contract basis by the various general stores in the town, which had more than ample stock because of the long lag between orders and deliveries in this remote outpost.

At noon, Engineer Webster believed matters were well enough in hand so that he could send a message to Lieutenant Carlin to bring the men of the *Vandalia* ashore. The word reached Lieutenant Carlin aboard the *Trenton* just at about the time that Admiral Kimberly was making the decision that the *Trenton's* crew, too, would abandon ship because the flagship was not salvageable.

The *Vandalia's* men were sent ashore first in the canoes of Mataafa and his men, and after they had left the ship, the men of the *Trenton* debarked, the powder division leaving first.

As the movement ashore began, it was already certain that Consul Blacklock was sitting on top of a powder keg, and he became so seriously worried about it that he communicated with the busy Admiral that very afternoon. Since early morning the day before, the grounds of the American consulate had been jammed with sailors who were treated, fed, and given hot coffee, even though there was no room for most of them inside. They had gone wandering up and down the streets of Apia—a matter of some consequence when a hundred or more sailors so wandered. But with the coming ashore of the crews of *Vandalia* and *Trenton* there would be some seven hundred Americans on the beach, with a Marine guard of only twenty-five men to control them.

Consul Blacklock asked for help.

Admiral Kimberly received the message in the early hours of the afternoon aboard the *Trenton* and appreciated the gravity of the situation. Immediately he took two actions: he dispatched Captain R. W. Huntington, chief of the Marine guard of the *Trenton,* with an additional force of fifty men to keep order in Apia; he also sent word to Captain Fritze, who was by this time resting ashore, that he would appreciate any effort the German naval forces might care to make to add to the military policing. Captain Fritze considered the request, then realized that the American military more than doubled his force of available men and that it would be most unwise to have the Germans so exposed. He replied that he would prefer to have the Americans take total responsibility for order in Apia for the moment.

During the afternoon, matters grew worse, instead of better, and Consul Blacklock took what seemed to him to be a desperate action. He issued an order to all saloon keepers in Apia—German, English, and American—telling them that they were forbidden to serve liquor to sailors of any nationality. If any liquor dealer disobeyed the order, Consul Blacklock said, a Marine guard would close his establishment, and all his liquor would be emptied into the street.

Then, and only then, did order begin to return to the streets of Apia.

CHAPTER NINETEEN

The Wreckage

Two somber tasks faced the surviving sailors of Germany and America when they came ashore on the morning of March 17th: to bind up their wounded and to count and bury their dead. Separately, as if they had not been occupying the two ends of the same long street, the Germans and Americans set about the unhappy work.

The German survivors were taken to The Old Firm's warehouse in Matafele, on the western side of the Mulivai, almost in the village of Savala. The Americans were quartered at the other end of the town. German doctors treated German wounded, and Germans and Samoans picked up German corpses for burial; American doctors and burial parties took care of their own; and the two forces had no direct contact with one another, but sat, like the two small, battered armies they were, at opposite ends of the ruined street.

When Commander Mullan reported to the Admiral that the *Nipsic* was in fair condition, he was ordered to round up his crew and get them back aboard that ship, where they were to remain, without shore leave; Lieutenant Brown, the navigator of the *Trenton,* was placed in charge of the men of that ship; Lieutenant Carlin continued in command of the men of the *Vandalia*.

Among the Germans, Captain Fritze took the handful of survivors of the *Eber* under his personal command and ordered them moved to the warehouse at Matafele. Captain von Erhardt came ashore briefly, noted the overcrowding and the confusion, conferred with Captain Fritze on his sickbed, and returned to the *Olga* with his entire crew.

So it was standoff.

The Americans were ashore with nearly nine hundred men, but the Germans were in possession of the only vessel that might still be called a fighting ship. True, the ship was aground, but her guns could still be run out to command the harbor.

These were all matters of consideration for the Germans and the Americans in Apia. Ironically, the people of Samoa, those whose futures were in doubt, who were at war with the Germans, were the only people on Upolu who had forgotten the political situation that existed three days before.

Even before the men of the warships were put ashore, the Samoans were helping secure the wreckage and salvaging what could be saved. They dragged huge sails from the water, such large sails that it took a dozen men to get them up. They went aboard the *Vandalia* and began to dismantle and haul her gun. They brought in barrels of provisions, some of which were yet good. They stacked tools and rifles and piles of rope and wood on the beach. No guards were needed; few Samoans were of a mind to steal the belongings of any others, and when stolen goods were discovered, they were returned and the thieves were punished by Mataafa's chiefs.

Even the Germans had nothing to fear from the people with whom they were at war. Consul Knappe was amazed, but within a few hours he had accepted the strange turn of events, and to show his gratitude he said he would pay the

Samoans who saved the lives of German seamen. He offered three dollars a head.

"I have saved three Germans," said one Samoan warrior. "I will make you a present of the three."

The first task of the Americans, order having been assured, was to treat the wounded; the counting of the dead could wait a few hours. The consulate was to continue as temporary hospital, with Fleet Surgeon Charles H. White in charge; Surgeon Derr gladly yielded the responsibility he had held for twenty-four hours; Surgeon Harvey of the *Vandalia,* who had spent ten hours clinging to the foretop, went to the hospital to work, but he broke down completely and had to be removed to bed himself; Surgeon Cordeiro, hampered by his displaced kneecap, could do nothing the first day, but on the second day he was carried into the hospital on a chair and began caring for ambulatory cases.

Nearly every man who had weathered the storm in the rigging of the *Vandalia* had been more or less seriously wounded. There were dozens of cases of inflamed eyes from the sand that flew through the air for so many hours. Many men suffered fractures to legs and arms; one seaman could not walk because his feet had been so badly lacerated by the ratlines. There were cases of dislocations and serious burns of men of the black gang who had been thrown against pipes or scalded by steam.

At the end of the day, however, the less seriously injured were discharged to duty, but eleven men of the *Vandalia* and three of *Trenton* were kept on in the hospital.

By midafternoon on the day of rescue, the crew of *Vandalia* had assembled in the old church, and the crew of the *Trenton* had been brought into homemade tents in a large lot near the center of the town. Admiral Kimberly saw the last of the men off the ship, and then he left the *Trenton,* which was filled with water up to the berth deck, putting her in the charge of Seumanu Tafa. The Admiral established his headquarters in the house of an American resident on the beach road not far from the consulate.

At six o'clock that evening, the men were mustered ashore and the orders for the military government under which they would live were read to them and then posted in their new quarters. Most stringent of the orders was one occasioned by the behavior of the men of the *Nipsic:* any seaman who refused to answer the challenge of a Marine guard would be shot on sight.

As to the dead, Germans and Americans began the mournful count. The *Eber* had gone down with sixty-six sailors and five officers; five survivors had been cast in by the storm, and four other seamen had been ashore for one reason or another. The *Adler* had lost twenty men and no officers, all the dead having gone over the side during the initial crash when the ship turned on her beam ends.

The *Vandalia* had suffered the greatest loss of any American ship: four officers, including her Captain, and thirty-nine men. Through panic the *Nipsic* had lost seven men; two civilian sailors had been lost from the schooner *Lily* when *Nipsic* ran her down; two Samoans had died heroes' deaths, risking their lives to save the men of the *Vandalia;* and aboard the *Trenton* one man had been killed when a port stove in.

So the storm had claimed 146 lives, sacrifices to the gods of nations and of pride. Nor was the tension in Apia particularly diminished by the lesson nature had tried to teach. The ships were gone or disabled, but the men were ashore, divided into two armed camps a mile apart, under an uneasy military law, the Americans remaining at their end of the town and the Germans staying on German property.

During that first day the basic problem for Admiral Kimberly was to get the men ashore safely and under rule of law; there could not be much thought of salvage until the next day. The men of the *Nipsic* might have been so employed, but they were scarcely trustworthy, and better off aboard their ship, where they got up steam and began sullenly to secure the decks under the eyes of their officers. That very day, two seamen deserted the ship.

The Admiral had no time to worry about the morale problems on the *Nipsic;* he was too busy with greater affairs. Bodies of seven Americans were buried that first day; on the second, more than a score of bodies were washed ashore and had to be cared for. In the struggle between Germans and others of the past three months the government of the town of Apia had collapsed completely. The worst problem this presented was in garbage and sewage control; the streams and alleys were choked with vegetation, and the Admiral feared an epidemic with so many more humans suddenly come ashore. Immediately, work parties were sent out to begin cleaning up the mess, and Mataafa's men were enlisted to help them. The waters of the Vaisingano were found to be polluted, but a search party discovered a clean spring, which became the American water supply.

The officers of the various ships found quarters where they could, some living with Samoan residents and some in the tents and barracks in the warehouse. Within twenty-four hours a routine had been established: the Admiral's flag flew over the camp, and an officer of the day kept military discipline.

Sunday, March 17th, was devoted to salvage of as much from *Trenton* as was possible, and most of this work was in the hands of the Samoans, who could dive like porpoises and swim like sharks. Enough provisions were salvaged to give the men regular fare of fresh and salt beef, canned meats, salmon, rice, hardtack, salt fish, beans, tea, coffee, sugar, pickles, and plum duff. From the shore they would have fresh pork, fresh bread made by a German baker, coconuts, limes, and breadfruit. There should have been bananas and oranges, too, but the banana trees and the orange groves had been destroyed by the storm.

On Monday, March 18th, the salvage continued, with emphasis still on the *Trenton,* lest she break up before her goods could be taken ashore. Sailers and Samoans got down the first whaleboat, the steam cutter, the sailing launch, and the third, fourth, and fifth cutters. They brought ashore small arms and ammunition, the Gatling gun, howitzers, and cabin furniture, which was stored in warehouses ashore. Time would now permit, so the Admiral instructed the men to save everything possible.

As the routine was established ashore, all appeared to be secure. The men arose at 6:30 and ate breakfast at 7. They cleaned their barracks and carried out their housekeeping duties until eight o'clock, when they were mustered and marched to the beach. They broke at twelve noon for lunch, then worked until late afternoon, when they were marched back to the barracks and given their evening meal. Captain Huntington was put in charge of the police of the town of Apia, as well as of the Marine guard, and Mataafa supplied policemen to assist him. Six revolvers, 180 pistol cartridges, five cutlasses, and five boarders' belts were served out from *Trenton*'s store to the men of *Vandalia,* and *Vandalia* was detailed to furnish four Marines for patrol. The patrol and all officers of all ships were authorized to arrest all disorderly persons.

On that second day after the storm, the men of the *Nipsic* were again too busy to cause trouble: Admiral Kimberly had ordered Commander Mullan to clear *Nipsic*'s decks, secure her, and make ready for a survey to decide whether she could be salvaged. At low water *Nipsic* was lying on her starboard bilge, heeled over 14 degrees, but with the rise of the tide she came up level; during the middle watch, she leaked about five inches of water, but the fires were going in two boilers, and the steam pumps kept the water down.

On the morning watch, Captain Mullan put his men to clearing the wreckage. The sailing launch was put over the side. The stream anchor was gotten up from the hold. The seamen fished the mainmast and sent the main topmast ashore, along with the main topsail yard. As the water went down, *Nipsic* heeled back to a 10-degree list on her starboard bilge.

As the men of the *Nipsic* worked to save their ship, and the other Americans and Samoans salvaged what they could from *Trenton* and *Vandalia,* the British man-of-war *Calliope* steamed up to Apia harbor during the evening, but did not enter the harbor until day dawned on March 19th.

Even if she had escaped the dangers of the harbor during the storm, *Calliope* had suffered a rough passage, and she showed it. Her jib boom was carried away, her bobstay, bands, and other fastenings of the bowsprit were gone, the foreyard was damaged, and her ornamental work at bow and stern was destroyed, as were some of the ouside fittings.

After noon on Saturday, when she had disappeared outside the arms of the reef, *Calliope* had steamed steadily toward the south, but she had not managed to make more than a knot against the storm, although her engines were working at 15-knot capacity. The wind had *increased* as she moved south; Captain Kane had serious worries about the ability of his ship to ride out the storm at sea, if it grew any worse. The weather was "thick as pea soup," and Captain Kane could not tell for hours whether he was ten miles off the reef or a few yards away. The wind blew thus until after eight o'clock that Saturday night, when *Calliope* passed through the worst of the storm (it continued a hurricane in Apia for another eight hours), but it was noon Sunday before Captain Kane had caught a glimpse of the sun.

On Sunday morning it had been far too rough to hold church services, but in the afternoon the chaplain held a short service of thanksgiving. The men of *Calliope* had much to be thankful for, and they knew it: Lieutenant McAlpine had been nearly swept off the topgallant forecastle and washed overboard while supervising the repair of the fore-yard; a block had struck him squarely in the face and knocked out a tooth. Lieutenant Carter was relieved after the middle watch, but instead of going below, he went to the knight-heads to watch the cables, and he was nearly crushed by the bowsprit when it carried away. Boatswain William Marshfield had stayed on the forecastle, watching over the anchor chains, until he was bruised and battered.

Calliope steamed into harbor on Tuesday morning with torn sails and battered spars and her paintwork much the worse for wear. Anchoring there with his single remaining anchor, the Captain stopped for a moment to give due credit to his crew for saving the ship. The lower deck was cleared, and every man was ordered aft to hear him speak.

He stood up, strong emotion masking his voice, and thanked them for their efforts, then told them what they must now do, tired and worn as they were. *Calliope* could not stay in Apia harbor; the Captain did not feel that the weather had yet settled, and he knew that if another storm arose, his ship could not survive it, with only one anchor.

He intended to leave the harbor as soon as *Calliope* had coaled, to make his way to Sydney for repairs. He asked the men to give him more of themselves, to hasten the coaling and get under way; then he thanked them again, mentioning names and deeds, until he was overcome with emotion and could not go on. Thereupon Bo'sun Marshfield blew his pipe and shouted:

"Disperse; quarters, clean guns."

The ceremony was over. It was back to the business of the sea.

Captain Kane went ashore that very day in his gig, to negotiate for coal and to pay calls on the various officials in the town. He passed by the wreck of *Vandalia,* where Samoan divers were trying to recover the safe. They did recover it that day, and salvaged $4,200 for the Paymaster's department.

The British Captain went first to the offices of MacArthur and Company, seeking coal, but none could be supplied; the pier, the lighters, and nearly all the coal on hand had been swept away by the storm. Captain Kane had no recourse, then, but to buy coal from The Old Firm at £4 6s 0d a ton, a price at least twice as high as he believed it should be. Yet he needed the coal and bought 150 tons.

His next call was on Captain Fritze at the German naval headquarters in Matafele. Captain Fritze was hardly up and about. He had suffered a severe concussion in the blow that knocked him to the deck when the *Adler* struck, and he was still chilly and weak, so weak that Captain Kane conducted his business with Captain von Erhardt, the commander of the *Olga* and second German officer in Samoa.

What could he do for them? Captain Kane asked the Germans.

He could take Lieutenant Emsmann of the *Olga* to Sydney with dispatches for the German naval headquarters in Berlin. Also, if Berlin approved Captain Fritze's request for help to the *Olga,* Captain Kane could hire a suitable steamer to come to Apia to assist the cruiser.

That was no problem at all, said Captain Kane, and he told Lieutenant Emsmann to make himself ready to sail.

Captain Kane then visited the American naval headquarters at the MacArthur warehouse, paid his call on Admiral

Kimberly, and offered his services again. They talked for a moment about the salute the Americans had given the British crew as they steamed out of Apia, at a time when the Americans might have been thinking of themselves alone. Captain Kane had been nearly overcome by the gesture, and he said as much. Nonsense, said the Admiral, he was as proud of the British ship's success as if it had been a ship of his own. He repeated an earlier remark of Admiral Josiah Latnall made under similar circumstances: "Blood is thicker than water."

The one thing the British could do for their cousins, said Admiral Kimberly, was to have *Calliope*'s divers examine *Nipsic*'s bottom to see if it was sound. So that very day Captain Kane sent his divers below to look, and they reported that *Nipsic* was sound as far as they could see. Admiral Kimberly was a careful man, however, and he asked Captain Kane whether it would be possible to let the Americans either buy or borrow the *Calliope*'s diving rig, so Captain Kane sent over a pump and two diving suits.

After his military calls, Captain Kane visited Consul de Coetlogon and told him that he must leave for Sydney. British and other residents complained that the *Calliope* should stay on to help, but actually there was little she could do, and Captain Kane was itching to be off.

The loading of stores and coal aboard the *Calliope* began.

That same day, Tuesday, Mataafa's men were helping the Germans wreck the *Adler*, taking ashore everything valuable in her that could be moved, for it was apparent that she could never be taken off the reef. (Her hulk still lies there, bleached and battered, a constant warning to sailors who venture into Apia harbor.)

In the morning, Lieutenant Hawley, the executive officer of *Nipsic*, took charge of the efforts to refloat the ship. Before eight o'clock in the morning, kedges had been carried out astern. An attempt was made to heave in the starboard bower chain, but it was discovered that the forefoot of the ship was resting on the chain, so the attempt was abandoned.

Between eight o'clock and noon, Hawley and his crew ran out two backed stream anchors with a heavy hawser and a line to the wreckage of *Vandalia*'s bowsprit, hoping thus to warp the ship off shore. The gunnery gang was put to work stripping the battery and overhauling the small arms, which had been thoroughly wetted by the sea.

At 8:45 that morning, the officer of the deck mustered the crew—and it was discovered that thirteen men were absent without leave. Later in the day, three of these men were brought aboard by the Marine guard from shore; the three were placed in the charge of the master at arms and slapped into the brig.

The crew were becoming hard to control, so later in the day Marine Sergeant Grupp and Private Chandler were brought back aboard to help maintain order on the ship. Lieutenant Hawley could not concern himself altogether with this problem of discipline, for it was his task to save the ship itself.

Late on Tuesday afternoon, the working gang of the *Nipsic* and a crew of Samoans brought a timber raft alongside, and the foreyard and the broken piece of the smokestack were taken off the ship. With pumping and securing, the list of the *Nipsic* had been reduced from 14 degrees to 5 degrees, and she had been pulled out until at low water the depth over the stern was twelve feet.

Captain Farquhar, Commander Mullan, and Lieutenant Carlin met at headquarters that afternoon to sit as a board of inquiry into the disaster. They reported that *Vandalia* was so far gone that her wardroom was filling with sand. Divers had confirmed Captain Farquhar's opinion that the back of *Trenton* was broken in two places, so she could not be saved. As for *Nipsic*, she was badly damaged, but she could be floated off and saved. The Admiral had wondered whether she could be made seaworthy enough to go to Honolulu or San Francisco, and Captain Mullan said she could not—she must be towed or convoyed to some closer, leeward port, such as Auckland, if she could move at all, he said. He doubted if she could be made seaworthy.

Ashore, there were troubles among the Americans of *Trenton* and *Vandalia;* four men were arrested for being out of bounds, three others were arrested for being out after taps (all of which were minor offenses), but two others were arrested for drunkenness, two for drunkenness and fighting, one for stealing, and one for refusing to obey orders. Yet these were small troubles compared to those aboard the *Nipsic:* at every muster, between a half-dozen and a dozen men were found to be missing, and some were declared to be out-and-out deserters from the ship. One of the worst offenders was a seaman, John McGowan, who was finally captured, brought back, and put in the brig in double irons.

Wednesday, March 20th, was the day of test for the *Nipsic.* It was a bright, sunny day with a very light breeze blowing from the southwest. All day long, lines were put out to the *Vandalia,* and attempts were made to warp the ship astern. She moved, but oh, so slowly. At eight o'clock in the morning, there was fifteen feet of water under the stern, but only eleven feet forward, and she was still aground. Three native divers bobbed around the boat, looking for anchor chains to which they could fix lines, and the *Calliope's* diver went below to examine the hull from one end to the other.

At four o'clock in the afternoon, Lieutenant Hawley ordered the unshipping of the boat davits on the starboard side and sent a line from the port bow to the wreck of one of the schooners on the eastern shore of the Vaisingano. At about 5:30, fifty Samoans came on shore to haul on cables and pull the ship off the beach. Twenty minutes later the heaving began; at 6:25 the *Nipsic* began to move, and did move until she brought up against wreckage under the bowsprit of *Vandalia*. The problem then—and it had to be solved before a squall upset every plan—was to haul *Nipsic* clear of the wreckage. In order to put more weight into the stern, where the water was deepest, Lieutenant Hawley ordered the 9-inch guns run aft. It was done, but with a casualty—one of the Samoans had his foot crushed under a truck.

The work had reached a critical point; *Nipsic* was neither aground nor safely afloat, and she was at the mercy of the slightest bit of weather. On the days before, the kedging and hauling had stopped at dark, but not this night, for the danger was too great. No one knew now when the wind might kick up, and the officers of the watch kept a sharp eye on the barometer. It was high enough, and the weather was warm and comfortable, yet it was a measure of the ordeal through which the men of the *Nipsic* had passed that when the barometer fell from 29.84 at nine o'clock in the morning to 29.74 at four o'clock in the afternoon, everyone began to grow a little edgy, and Lieutenant Hawley decided to work through the night, if necessary.

At eight o'clock a line was warped over to the *Olga,* and shortly afterward, when the heaving began again, *Nipsic* came off the beach and was truly afloat.

Lieutenant Hawley stopped the work at 9:30 and sent the Samoans ashore. The moonlight shone brightly on a harbor that was completely quiet and as smooth as glass.

CHAPTER TWENTY

The Way Home

A LIEUTENANT HAWLEY and his men struggled to float the *Nipsic,* the remaining boats of *Trenton* were at work, along with Samoan boats and those of *Calliope,* lightering the 150 tons of coal the British ship needed for her voyage. As much as anything else, Admiral Kimberly was glad to help the British out just to keep the men of *Trenton* and *Vandalia* busy. This matter of occupation for some seven hundred men would be a serious worry for the next few weeks, until ships could come from the mainland to bring home the shipwrecked crews.

On Wednesday afternoon the mail schooner sailed from Apia to Tutuila so that it could meet the steamer that would be traveling from San Francisco to Auckland. Admiral Kimberly sent Lieutenant Wilson on board and instructed him to go to Auckland, cable his dispatches to Washington by way of London, and, if possible, charter a steamer to take the American sailors back to the United States.

By Wednesday midnight the coal was loaded aboard *Calliope* and she was ready to leave. Captain Kane waited until early Thursday morning, and at 7:30 weighed anchor, heading for Sydney. *Caliope* fired a salute of 13 guns in honor of Admiral Kimberly and the American flag, and then stood out to sea; as the anchor came up and the ship began to move, the Captain saw *Nipsic* finally freed from the wreckage near *Vandalia*. Early in the morning, Lieutenant Hawley had moved her out into deep water, clear of the *Trenton*.

Off Salauafata, *Calliope* encountered the mail schooner, with Lieutenant Wilson aboard—and it was good that she saw the little ship, because the schooner had lost a keel badly battered by the storm, and she was beating about against a light wind, getting absolutely nowhere. Captain Kane took her in tow and pulled her to the anchorage off Tutuila; had he not seen her, Lieutenant Wilson would have missed the mail steamer, and the first word the United States would have had of the disaster at Apia would have been secondhand information given out by the British.

As it was, ten days elapsed after departure from Apia before Lieutenant Wilson reached Auckland and filed his dispatches at the cable office, along with the reports of the Associated Press correspondent and other newspapermen on Apia.

The cable carried the word in time for the morning newspapers of the West Coast to have the story on Saturday morning, March 30th, although most Eastern readers did not learn of the disaster until the following morning.

Americans were stunned; the war talk that had been flooding the country was suddenly stilled. In Washington, Navy Secretary Tracy cabled Lieutenant Wilson for Admiral Kimberly, giving the Admiral full power to do as he wished about the men of the *Vandalia* and the *Trenton*. He informed the Admiral, also, that the U.S.S. *Monongahela* had sailed for Apia on February 21.

As the newspapers pointed out, it was the greatest disaster the American Navy had ever suffered in time of peace, and in recent years there had been few disasters nearly so serious.

In Washington the families of the naval officers began to congregate at the Navy Department. One of the first to arrive was Mrs. Reamy, wife of one of the *Trenton*'s lieutenants, tearful and worried. Captain Mullan's brother was another visitor that day; dozens of people with no apparent Navy business thronged along the corridors, even though it was Sunday.

As to the drumbeaters of a few weeks earlier, they were strangely silent; Admiral Porter, sought out by a reporter, flatly refused to talk, which was completely unlike him. Commodore Walker, superintendent of the Bureau of Ships, was persuaded to say that the loss meant $2,500,000 to the United States Navy in the value of the ships alone; more he would not say.

The New York World, which had an abiding interest in promoting trouble and excitement in Samoa, sent a correspondent to interview Commodore Walker, and so did *The Washington Post*. The newspapermen wondered how many warships would be dispatched immediately to Samoa, but they were told that none would be. (The *Monongahela* was an old stores ship, armed only with a few howitzers that provided dubious self-protection.) The fighting ship *Mohican* was at Panama, said the Commodore, and the man-of-war *Alert* was at Honolulu; the more modern *Iroquois* and *Adams* were in the yards at Mare Island, but no plans had been made to send any of them to Samoa.

Back in Apia, Admiral Kimberly had matters under better control every day. He was indefatigable in his personal direction of the affairs on shore and was as excited as a cadet when he learned that the *Nipsic* was again afloat.

On March 21st, after the ship was floated into deep water, the divers from the *Trenton,* using the *Calliope*'s gear, made a complete report on the condition of the hull. She hardly leaked at all; three propeller blades were twisted and bent, and one blade was broken; sails and hawsers had fouled the propeller; the connection between the sternpost and the rudderpost had carried away, and the rudderpost and the rudder had been lost; the false keel was broken off, and two strakes of copper were missing; the copper had come off the bilge in places, but the planks themselves were not bulged or broken; all the copper plating had come off the bow, and off other parts of the hull, but generally speaking, the hull was sound.

When Admiral Kimberly learned this news, he was both jubilant and annoyed; pleased with the information that at least one of his ships was saved, but upset over the gloomy prognostications of Commander Mullan and that officer's poor showing. The Admiral then took matters out of Commander Mullan's hands. Lieutenant Commander Lyon was put to work supervising the overall work on the *Nipsic,* and it began to move apace. A steady stream of material flowed to the gunboat: oars, spars, lumber, brass, belaying pins, tarpaulins, and hammock cloths from the two sunken ships. The divers picked up four anchors from the bottom and put them aboard the ship. (One was a German anchor from the *Adler,* which was later returned.) The *Nipsic* was re-rigged and given a jury rudder. The smokestack of *Vandalia* was salvaged and went to replace the broken stack of *Nipsic.*

As soon as the emergency was over, Mataafa came down from the mountains to visit Admiral Kimberly. The Admiral said he needed men to salvage materials from the *Vandalia* and *Trenton,* and Mataafa put a hundred Samoan warriors at the disposal of the Americans for as long as they might be needed. Soon the Samoans were at work, alongside the Americans, removing the guns of the ships. Every day the sailors came down, led by the *Trenton*'s band, which played while the men worked.

All during the first week after the storm, the bodies of the drowned men kept washing ashore. Pay Clerk Roche's body was found and buried at Mulinuu point, and the next day Paymaster Arms's body was found at Matautu and was buried there. Captain Schoonmaker's body came ashore at the Vailele plantation, four miles east of the harbor, and was buried there by Manager Haidlen.

While Mataafa was in Apia, he sent gifts to the Americans, sleeping mats for the sailors in their tents and barracks, and coconuts and other fruits. He toured the tent camp and noted that the tents were leaking in the rain that fell at least once every day. He then offered to have every Samoan in Apia give up his house and live in the woods, so the Americans might have better accommodation, but Admiral Kimberly said he could not control his men if they were so widely scattered, and the offer was refused.

On March 24th the American schooner *Equator* arrived in Apia, and Admiral Kimberly decided to send the cadets from *Trenton* and *Vandalia* on her to intercept the mail steamer *Alameda*, which would take the youngsters back to San Francisco. They climbed aboard, eleven of them, although there were accommodations only for four, and nested down in the stinking cargo of copra. But after a day or two, the schooner intercepted the mail ship and the first of the survivors of the great typhoon set out on their voyage home.

CHAPTER TWENTY-ONE

Materials for an Incident

IN APIA, one day of drudgery followed another, or so it seemed to the crews of the American ships who were stranded on this foreign shore without their usual food, camping under strange conditions, and allowed none of the recreation they usually enjoyed on shore. For Admiral Kimberly the wreck of the international fleet had simply changed the nature of his mission slightly, and not for a moment, even as he personally supervised the refitting of the *Nipsic,* did the Admiral forget that mission.

Ten days after the hurricane, Mataafa sent a letter to Admiral Kimberly, asking him to intervene and persuade the Tamasese men to disband their army and go home, now that the protecting German warships were no longer the key force in Apia. That same day, Admiral Kimberly called on German Consul Knappe to ascertain the German attitude.

Knappe assured him (as he had assured so many others) that the Germans wanted nothing but peace and cooperation in Samoa. The Admiral visited the American consulate, where Consul Blacklock warned him not to believe what the Germans said—they would not give up their support of

Tamasese until they were sure they could not win the struggle. A few days later, when the mail came in from Tutuila, it brought news of the recall of Dr. Knappe as German Consul, but under the circumstances, the news was not very warming: he was to be replaced by Dr. Steubel, a former consul at Apia who had stirred up much of the trouble in the earlier days. Consul Blacklock remarked that this was not a sign of peace, but rather a German sign of defiance to the United States at a moment when the Kaiser had not the force to fight. Steubel had come to Samoa in 1883, and he had in three years laid the foundation for all the troubles that had led to war. That news, plus the report that the Germans were sending more ships and 2,000 men to Samoa, gave the Americans cause for new worry.

On March 29th the Germans brought 150 of Tamasese's warriors down to the beach under protective guard so there would be no incident with the Mataafa men, and they helped float off the *Olga,* which was found to be sound and, in the Admiral's eyes, capable of a sea voyage. Two days later, the German steamer *Lubeck* arrived. At first, the Americans feared that the 2,000 German troops would be aboard that steamer, but they were relieved to discover no replacements at all.

On April 2nd the *Lubeck* and *Olga* sailed to Sydney. Captain Fritze and all the officers and men of the German squadron left with the ships, save four officers and eighty sailors who remained as an armed guard at the German consulate.

Admiral Kimberly and Consul Blacklock were puzzled as to the German intentions, but they need not have been— those intentions were exactly the same that they had been for several years: to dominate Samoa. The Germans were simply awaiting the coming of the new German squadron before taking aggressive action.

When the Germans sailed, Mataafa's men went out in

search of the Tamasese force to do battle, but they did not find the other army, and the weather closed in on them, preventing further hostilities for several days.

On April 8th, Associated Press reporter Dunning called at the German consulate for an interview, and Dr. Knappe told him that the war between Germany and Mataafa was still on, that the German ships would soon arrive in Apia, and then the fireworks would begin.

Chief Patu, a Mataafa supporter, learned of this interview and went to Dr. Knappe to see whether the German Consul would confirm it. If so, he said, Mataafa would not wait for the coming of the Germans, but would hunt down and kill all the Tamasese troops immediately, then dispose of every German ashore and seize all German property.

Dr. Knappe reversed himself. He begged the Chief to go back to Mataafa and tell him that Germany was no longer at war with the Samoans, that the Consul knew absolutely nothing about any more ships coming, and that there would be no more fighting. (At the same time, in Berlin there were reports that the cruiser *Sperber* and the corvette *Alexander*, two of Germany's most modern warships, had been dispatched to Samoa.)

On April 12th the last gun was brought ashore from the *Trenton,* and the entire battery was lined up outside the Samoan government building, an obvious warning to the Germans. The British steamer *Mawhera* arrived, and Admiral Kimberly decided that work had come far enough along on the *Nipsic* so that she could be sent back to Auckland for further repairs. Most of the serious damage to the exterior had been repaired; the engines had been bent and twisted, as had many pipes, and the floor plates in the fire room would not go into place; but much of this, too, had been corrected. The jury rudder had been rigged: a long wide blade that hung out astern, fixed to a spar which stuck out over the after part of the poop deck, with tackles on each end of the spar rove to the wheel so *Nipsic* would steer.

The *Mawhera* brought a New Zealand shipbuilder who had hoped to make a killing by salvaging some of the wrecked warships in the harbor. He called on Admiral Kimberly, who gave him free run of the American camp and asked his advice. The shipbuilder looked over *Trenton* and said she could be gotten off and rebuilt, but he agreed with the Admiral that the expense would be so great it was not worth while. He looked over *Nipsic* and said there should be no trouble about getting her to Auckland safely.

With this remark, the shipbuilder stepped into the middle of a serious controversy that had been raging in the American camp. For reasons of prestige, the Admiral was most eager to have the *Nipsic* steam to the outside world under her own power. Captain Mullan and several of his officers had been grumbling all the while, and they now came out openly to claim that the ship was not seaworthy and should not be taken out of Apia. Until the shipbuilder came to reinforce his view, the Admiral had been leery of giving a direct order, but his mind was made up, and he ordered Captain Mullan to coal and prepare for sea. Further, he said, the Captain was to order his officers to stop talking about the unsafe condition of the ship. (This was more than a gentle hint to the Captain himself.)

Captain Mullan's orders were to have the ship repaired at Auckland and then to return to Pago Pago.

On April 17th *Nipsic* weighed anchor and steamed out of the harbor, to be followed by *Mawhera.*

The gunboat had scarcely cleared the outer edges of the reef when a squall blew up. As the squall caught *Nipsic,* Captain Mullan ordered her headed into the wind, and the strain of turning the ship so rapidly caused the spar to break on the port end. Suddenly, the steering gear was gone.

Just at this time, Engineer Hall reported that the engines were not functioning properly and must be shut down, or there was danger that they would be wrecked altogether. The realignment, done in Apia harbor without docking or engineering facilities, had been less than proper.

The engines were stopped. What happened next was reminiscent of the terrible days of a month before; *Nipsic* began to drift in toward the western reef. Captain Mullan told his engineer that he must get the engines repaired at least enough for some use and put the deck crew to work setting sail to bring the ship's head into the wind. After a trying half-hour the engines were repaired enough for use, and *Nipsic* steamed out to a position two miles off the reef; a signal had been made to *Mawhera,* and she came out to the rescue.

The voyage out had been triumphal; the voyage back was a miserable tow, at one knot.

When *Nipsic* came in that day, the controversy began all over again. Admiral Kimberly said the ship was sound and that she could make New Zealand under her own power and would do so just as soon as a new jury rudder could be rigged. Captain Mullan said the ship was unseaworthy.

CHAPTER TWENTY-TWO

War and Peace

O N THE DAY that Nipsic sailed out on her abortive voyage, exactly a month after the disastrous typhoon, Admiral Kimberly prepared a proclamation calling on the Samoans to put an end to the war among themselves. It was his first move to break German power.

Copies of the proclamation were sent all over the islands, and Captain Farquhar and Commander Mullan donned their full-dress uniforms, with swords, and went to Tamasese's camp to deliver the proclamations in person, to make a show of American power, and to convince Tamasese that he had best step down from his throne of pretentions.

Tamasese was noncommittal. The next day, a Mataafa chief came to the American consulate and told Consul Blacklock that on the very day of Captain Farquhar's mission to Tamasese, Consul Knappe had visited the Tamasese camp. The result of the meeting was an order to prepare for battle.

Admiral Kimberly was furious when he learned of this double-dealing by the Germans, and he called for an explanation from Consul Knappe. Not having a very large force ashore, the German Consul came immediately to the Admiral's headquarters and denied all.

No one believed him.

Early on the morning of April 23rd a party of Mataafa's men were giving safe escort to two Tamasese women through Mataafa country. The women had been visiting relatives in the Mataafa camp.

On the way, the Mataafa party was ambushed by Tamasese warriors who had known of the visit and had lain in wait for the party. The Mataafa men fought back, although two men were wounded, but finally had to retreat and escape by jumping into the sea.

Immediately Mataafa began preparation for a full-scale attack on Tamasese's camp. Only through Admiral Kimberly's effort was an immediate battle averted; Mataafa promised to keep the peace if his enemies would do so, and matters simmered thus for the next few days. The Admiral guaranteed the peace, then settled down to wait for instructions from Washington about the political and military situations, for word from the Navy Department about the official attitude toward the loss of two ships, and for the Germans to make the next move.

As the Admiral negotiated, Bismarck began to wield what little was left of his fading power, and he persuaded the Kaiser to reopen the Samoan three-power conference. As the Tamasese men attacked Mataafa's men, the American commissioners to a new conference at Berlin were on the high seas aboard the Cunard liner *Umbria,* and prominent among them was former Consul Sewall, who had worked so hard for Samoan freedom from German rule.

In Sydney, a jubilant Lieutenant Wilson had finally managed to charter the steamer *Rockton,* was fitting her up with mattresses, berths, and blankets for the accommodation of 450 men, and had bought provisions to feed his little army.

On April 29th, the *Rockton* arrived at Apia harbor, and that very day Admiral Kimberly decided to send home every man the steamer could take. The German contingent in Apia was less than a hundred men; no German warships had come into harbor; and it was the Admiral's understanding from Washington that the status of Samoa would hang in the balance at Berlin, so there was no point in keeping American sailors ashore and inactive. He would stay on, with a staff of ten officers and seventy-five men—quite enough to offset the Germans. The eight officers and 142 men of the *Vandalia* would go home, and so would twelve officers and three hundred men from the *Trenton. Nipsic* would remain in the harbor until repairs were completed, and then she would steam for a friendly port, unassisted.

Bright and early on the morning of May 1st, the harbor of Apia awakened to bustle and noise aboard the *Rockton,* and by nine o'clock the bay was filled with the canoes of Samoans coming to say goodbye to the Americans. There were two bands to play—that of the *Trenton,* which was leaving, and that of the British man-of-war *Rapid,* which had just steamed into port. Both bands played with a will for an hour and a half, and then it was time for *Rockton* to sail. At 10:30 the chains clanked and the anchor of the steamer was hauled aboard, the band of the *Rapid* played "Auld Lang Syne," the sailors of the *Nipsic* gave three cheers for their lucky comrades who were going home, and the crowds ashore and afloat waved flowers and shouted until they were hoarse as the big steamship put out to sea. It was a beautiful day, a day of bright blue sky and warming sun, with a gentle western breeze blowing over the flower-decked canoes, and only the lapping of the soft blue waves against the bleaching hull of *Adler* on the reef reminded a watcher that there had ever been a storm.

The *Rockton*'s whistle blasted, and she began to move;

on deck a few men strained to look to the left at Mulinuu, where Pay Clerk Roche rested in his grave, and to the right, where Paymaster Arms was buried beneath the waving palms of Matautu; then the ship was out of the mouth of Apia harbor, steaming east, to pass close by the grassy point at Vailele where the cross that marked the grave of Captain Schoonmaker stood, sentinel in the friendly sun, and heads were bowed in the memory of the brave men who had perished in the anger of the sea. The ship steamed on. Lieutenant Carlin alone looked back, for one long moment, and then turned around to look ahead toward America in the gathering sun.

Epilogue

THE *Rockton* arrived home safe and sound in San Francisco in a thick, dripping fog on the morning of May 20th, but the men of the typhoon had never seen a sight as welcome as the grim outline of Alcatraz and the brown hills of Sausalito. Captain Farquhar was there, a bit nervous because he had demanded a board of inquiry into the loss of his ship, lest he be shunted off, dishonored. Secretary of the Navy Tracy, however, would have none of it; instead, he sent and published a dispatch to Admiral Kimberly, praising in the highest terms the American officers and men who had fought through the hurricane winds of the typhoon and calling them heroes. An inquiry would be senseless, he said; the matter was officially closed.

Lieutenant Brown, the navigator of the *Trenton*, was there and happy as the rest, although in later years his career was to be marred by a dispute with Admiral Kimberly over Brown's conduct during the storm. The Lieutenant was seeking promotion in the undermanned and niggardly Naval Service and he went to Congress to press his case, claiming that *he* had saved the *Trenton* from outright disaster. Quite rightly, Admiral Kimberly pointed out that while Brown had done his duty, the Admiral and the Captain had been in charge, and the *Trenton* had been saved by many men.

Engineer Webster was there, and he was to go on to a long and distinguished career in his nation's service. Cadet Wiley was not there; he had gone on ahead with the other cadets a month before, to be much chagrined when assigned to the old *Adams* and sent back for further duty at Apia, but he overcame his chagrin, and eventually became an admiral. Lieutenant Carlin was there, and he, too, lived on to enjoy a distinguished naval career.

In Apia, Admiral Kimberly personally watched over the preparations of the *Nipsic* for sea. His arguments with Captain Mullan and the officers of the ship continued. On May 9th, she sailed for Auckland accompanied by the U.S.S. *Alert,* but in the heavy seas they encountered, Captain Mullan decided *Nipsic* was not seaworthy and brought her back to Apia harbor. Here, at his own request, he was relieved of command, and Lieutenant Commander Lyon was given the ship. On May 15th, the new Captain sailed out of Apia harbor and took *Nipsic* safely into Hawaii, stopping at Pago Pago and Fanning Island. There the ship was rebuilt and kept in service in the islands until the fall of 1890, when she was taken to the Mare Island naval shipyard and decommissioned.

At Berlin the three big powers agreed that Samoa was to remain independent. Dr. Stuebel did return to Apia as German Consul, but to carry out an entirely new policy of conciliation. King Laupepa, who had been taken around the world and confined in the Marshall Islands, was returned unharmed to his kingdom and resumed his throne with the blessing of Mataafa, and Tamasese sank into oblivion, soon to die. The Samoans laid down their arms and returned to the old easy way of life. In summing up, one might say that through the terrible forces of nature—the typhoon—peace came to Samoa, and, if one were of imaginative turn of mind and suspicious of the aims of nations, one might call the typhoon The Disaster That Saved the World.

Notes and Acknowledgments

The idea for this book was suggested in reading Robert Louis Stevenson's *A Footnote to History, Eight Years of Trouble in Samoa,* published by Charles Scribner's Sons in 1892, when the Samoan tragedy was fresh in the minds of Americans and the people of Europe. For the pointing up of the idea in its final form the author is very much indebted to editor Howard Cady.

The research material for the book came from various far-flung sources. Rear Admiral L. A. Kimberly's pamphlet, "Samoan Hurricane," published by the Naval Historical Foundation, was an important source. So was the personal narrative of Chief Engineer Harrie Webster, which was published in the October, 1894, issue of the *United Service* magazine. The Division of Naval History, Ship's History Section, Navy Department, supplied a history of the U.S.S. *Nipsic.* The meteorological data on the great storm came from the *United States Naval Institute Proceedings,* Vol. 17, No. 2, Whole Number 58, 1891, an article written by Marine Meteorologist Everett Hayden. Admiral Kimberly's official account of the storm and the loss of the American ships appeared in the Annual Report of the Secretary of the Navy for 1889, as housed in the Library of Congress. The story of the *Calliope* in Apia comes largely from British official documents, especially

NAVY H.M.S. *Calliope,* Report of the Hurricane at Samoa, Parliamentary Paper No. 5732 of 1889, published by Her Majesty's Stationery Office. Another vital source was a privately printed booklet detailing the first commission of H.M.S. *Calliope* by Captain E. W. Swan in which the official reports, documents, and various eyewitness accounts of the disaster were brought together. Another account of the *Calliope* appeared in *The Navy,* a British magazine, in December, 1951, under the pseudonym "Taffrail."

Part of the story of the sinking of *Vandalia* was told by Admiral Henry A. Wiley, U.S.N. (Ret.) in *An Admiral from Texas,* published by Doubleday, Doran and Co. at Garden City, N.Y., in 1934. Admiral Wiley was a naval cadet aboard the *Vandalia* in 1889.

Other documents include Navy Documents in the National Archives, the letters of Secretary of the Navy William C. Whitney relative to the ships involved, messages sent the *Trenton,* Admiral Kimberly, and others, the logs of the *Nipsic* and the *Trenton* for March and April, 1889. (The log of the *Vandalia* went down with the ship.) The United States Navy Library in Washington kindly furnished details on the construction and rigging of *Trenton, Vandalia,* and *Nipsic.* The Naval Historical Foundation papers in the Library of Congress comprise a number of interesting documents, including a letter of March 26, 1889, from Lieutenant J. W. Carlin to a friend in Hawaii, describing the sinking of the *Vandalia.* Captain John A. Gray, M.C., U.S.N., published an interesting book, *Amerika Samoa; A History of American Samoa and Its United States Naval Administration,* published by the U.S. Naval Institute, Annapolis, 1960. One chapter deals with the Apia hurricane of 1889.

The *Army and Navy Journal* of April 6, 1889, contained excellent background material about the ships and crews of the American squadron.

Other sources were: *Gods Who Die,* Julian Dana, New York, 1935; *Disasters at Sea,* the Mary E. Powell collection of the Library of Congress; the Papers of the Military History Society of Massachusetts, 1902, for an account of Admiral Kimberly's adventures; *New Zealand's Naval Story* by T. D. Taylor, A. H. and A. W.

Reed, Wellington, 1948; the dispatches from United States Consuls in Apia, December, 1888, to November, 1889, in the National Archives; *The Vengeful Sea,* by Edward Rowe Snow, Dodd, Mead and Co., 1956; *The Army and Navy Register,* Vol. 10, 1889.

For accounts of the German vessels in the Apia tragedy I leaned heavily on several publications in the Library of Congress: *Kanonenboot Eber vor Samoa, Ein deutscher Seemann erlebt die Kämpfe um Apia,* Ostfrid von Hanstein, Steiniger Verlage, Berlin, 1941; *Samoa,* Dr. F. Reinicke, Wilhelm Süsserat Verlagsbuchhandung, Berlin, 1902; and *Eisenschmidts Büchersammlung für Unteroffiziere und Mannschaften,* Korvettenkapitän Tessdorpf; also von OberMüller's *Samoa,* H. Mayers Verlag, Leipzig; and Thamm's *Von Kiel bis Samoa,* Conrads Verlag, Berlin.

Many newspaper accounts of the tragedy were consulted; most valuable of all of them was Associated Press Correspondent Dunning's long report on the tragedy, which appeared in hundreds of American newspapers on March 31, 1889, when the first news of it reached America.

I used *Der Deutsche Correspondent* of Baltimore, Md., for March and April, 1889; *The New York Times* of 1889, for all the first six months of the year; the *San Francisco Examiner,* March, April, May, 1889; the *San Francisco Chronicle,* March and April, 1889; *The Samoa Times,* March, April, 1889; *The New York Tribune,* for March and April, 1889, and the *Library of Tribune Extras,* July, 1889; *The New York World,* March and April, 1889; *The Washington Post,* March and April, 1889; the Washington *Evening Star,* March, 1889.

I am indebted to many librarians and others for a great deal of help all the way through the research, especially Dr. Arnold Price of the Library of Congress; those in the newspaper room at Harvard University's library; Librarian Greenwood of the United States Navy Library and his assistants; librarians at Scoville Memorial Library at Salisbury, Conn. I am also indebted to Olga G. Hoyt for translations from the German.

Bomoseen, Vermont
July 24, 1967

Index

Index

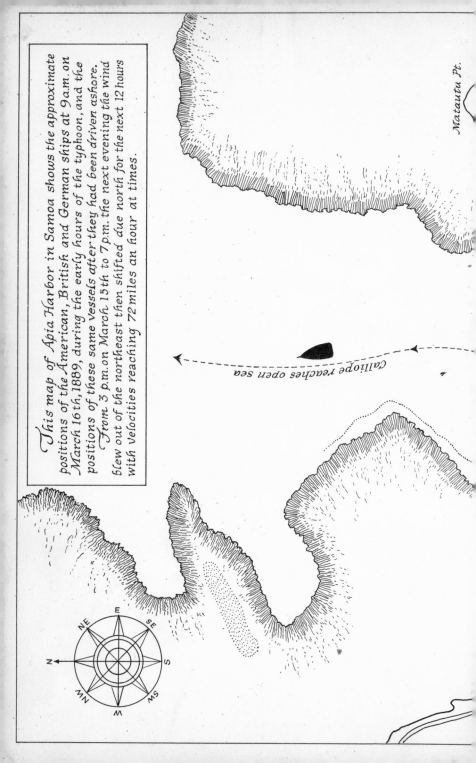

This map of Apia Harbor in Samoa shows the approximate positions of the American, British and German ships at 9 a.m. on March 16th, 1889, during the early hours of the typhoon, and the positions of these same vessels after they had been driven ashore.

From 3 p.m. on March 15th to 7 p.m. the next evening the wind blew out of the northeast then shifted due north for the next 12 hours with velocities reaching 72 miles an hour at times.

Matautu Pt.

Calliope reaches open sea